Behind Grandma's Apron Strings

Stories of God's Grace and Mercy

by

Robert Loran Ford

Copyright © 2014 Robert Loran Ford All Rights Reserved

His Way Publishing, Winston Salem, NC

Printed in the United States of America First Edition

For information about permission to reproduce selections

from this book, write to:

Robert L. Ford email address

Book design by Penworthy LLC

ISBN: 0970958013
EAN-13: 978-0-9709580-1-3

Scripture quotations, unless otherwise noted, are from the

King James Version of the Bible.

Dedication

I dedicate this book to my wife, Gail, who has always seen potential in me that I did not see for myself. When I have been faced with a challenge in my life, she has always pointed out my strengths as opposed to my doubts and fears of failure.

If she were not a part of my life, this book would never have happened. She has truly been my best friend and the love of my life.

Acknowledgments

Many people in my life have encouraged me to put some of my thoughts into print. I resisted this encouragement as long as I could, until it became apparent that I needed to do something to get them off my back.

The opportunity to write has come to me via a monthly newsletter at Mt Vernon Baptist Church in Vale, NC. The *Army Times* and the *Hickory Daily Record* have published some of my thoughts.

Although various family members and friends have given me good supportive feedback no one has given me more encouragement than my wife, Gail, who has reminded me over and over again that I should do this. Her persistence has paid off.

It is one thing to have a manuscript for a book and another to have the manuscript put into book form, so no one has been more helpful in this process than my lifelong college and seminary friend, Dennis Hester. He opened a whole new world of publishing for me that was a bit overwhelming at first, and helped me get through it.

To all the folks who have found their way into my life stories, I thank you for your friendship and for allowing me to be a part of your life's journey.

TABLE OF CONTENTS

Dedication	i
Acknowledgments	iii
Foreword	ix
Introduction	xi
1. Behind Grandma's Apron Strings	1
2. A Time of Struggle, Resistance, and Conflict	3
3. A Call in the Night	6
4. A Cliff Hanger	11
5. A Dog's Tail	14
6. A Man and His Dog	17
7. A Near Death Experience	20
8. A Ride that Won't Let Go	22
9. A Song, a Touch, and a Prayer	24
10. A Trip to the Beach	27
11. A Tug of War with the Dentist	30
12. Am I My Brother's Keeper?	33

13. Bad Things Happen	36
14. Behind Closed Doors	40
15. Bumps, Bruises, and Bicycles	43
16. Cauthman's Cat	45
17. Choosing Sides	47
18. Comfort, Comfort My People	50
19. Dragons, Giants, and Castles	52
20. Dreams of Success	55
21. Going To Nineveh	58
22. Growing Pains	63
23. Hide and Go Seek	67
24. Hope for the Hopeless	69
25. How Much Does It Cost?	73
26. Hub-Bah Hub-Bah Ice Cream	76
27. Hunting Squirrels	79
28. I Can't Do That!	82
29. Is This Equipment Necessary?	85
30. Just a Piece of Glass	89

31. Luck or Divine Intervention — 93

32. No Longer Needed — 97

33. Not Smart Enough — 102

34. Once I Was Blind, but Now I See — 105

35. Recovering from a Stall — 108

36. Slaves of Freedom — 111

37. Sometimes Smaller Is Better — 114

38. Surrounded by the Police — 117

39. Target Practice Gone Bad — 121

40. The Prodigal Finds Himself — 123

41. The Shoes Don't Fit — 126

42. The Short Life of Ernie Hawkins — 129

43. The Worst Student.110 — 132

44. Truth Has Consequences — 135

45. Waiting & Waiting & Waiting — 138

46. Which Way Is Home? — 141

47. Who Was That Masked Man? — 144

48. Wrestling with God on Hogback Mountain — 148

49. Cruising for a Bruising — 151

50. Which Way to Turn? — 154

Afterword — 157

RESOURCES — 159

Foreword

God is much easier to find than we think. God wants us to find Him and works to make Himself known.

Robert Ford's book, *Behind Grandma's Apron Strings*, reminds us that God is everywhere and wants to forgive and to meet our every need.

Through this book of devotionals, Robert shows that there are lessons to be learned in daily events. Using colorful reflections of dis- appointments, triumphs, sorrows and joys, he shows us that God wants to help us see Him in a different light. These reflections of God will inspire us to be believers and more faithful followers of Him.

When Robert faced the wrath and discipline of his grandfather, he hid behind his grandma's apron strings. What Robert found is what all of us are looking for from God. As struggling human beings, we long for God's grace and mercy. God has the power to destroy us, but longs to mold us into being His faithful people. Robert's stories will inspire us to see God everywhere.

When Robert preaches, he always has something worthy to say, and lives what he preaches. He cares for sinners and saints alike.

As you read these intimate slices of Robert's life you will

get to know Robert, but even more you will meet God and learn how much He wants to give what we so desperately need: His unconditional love, His bountiful forgiveness, and gracious mercy.

Dennis J. Hester

Author, Publisher and Fellow Minister, but more important, Bob's friend for more than 40 years

Introduction

It is often said that God works in mysterious ways in the world and in our personal lives. This devotional book contains stories throughout various chapters of my life and some of the events that I have viewed in the lives of those around me. I believe that often the activity of God goes unnoticed and undetected in the day-to-day operation of life. What I have set out to do is to take some of these events and point out how God is active when we are least aware of it.

On his first night away from home, Jacob dreamed of angels going up and down a large ramp. The next morning he exclaimed, "God was in this place and I knew it not." It is in looking back into our lives that we discover just how God has been active.

It is my belief that God is always active in every area of our lives, no matter how insignificant the situation may appear. It is my hope that you will connect with some of the stories and discover just how active God is in your daily life.

We, too, may discover that God does not forsake or leave us at any time. While we may feel alone in this busy world, we are never truly alone. God is always where He needs to be. He is always seeking to guide us from where we are to where we need to be.

The following 50 stories constitute my attempt to share with you how I see God at work in my life and the world around me. Like the shepherds on a hillside one night long ago, I have been surprised how God has touched me through these events.

1

Behind Grandma's Apron Strings

When I was only seven, my parents sent me off for the summer to stay with my grandparents on the farm. My grandparents' farm was located in the foothills of western North Carolina, among apple trees and a vast number of farm animals. You would think these would have been carefree and trouble free days for me, but not so.

There were a variety of things to do on the farm: apple trees to climb, a sugar cane patch to satisfy our sweet tooth and a watermelon patch with some of the best melons in the area. With all this at hand, how could anything go wrong?

The only downside to farm life was that there was only one bicycle, and it belonged to my Aunt Joyce. One day we had a little disagreement about whose turn it was to ride the bicycle. I was losing the argument and did something that I have since regretted. I picked up a green persimmon and threw it at my Aunt Joyce. It hit her square in the back, and she went running and crying to Grandpa.

Although I had not been on the farm that many days, I was well aware of the razor strap that hung next to the front door. I was also aware of what that razor strap was used for on the farm. My life flashed before my eyes; Grandpa was going to use that strap on me. Joyce was the youngest of eight children and Grandpa's favorite. There was no way I was going to get out of this mess.

So, I did the only thing I knew to do: I ran for Grandma. I found her in the kitchen and hid behind her apron strings as Grandpa entered the room. I thought I was a goner, but Grandma came to the rescue. She would not allow Grandpa to lay a hand on me.

Behind Grandma's apron strings, I found the grace that I needed. I deserved the whipping that Grandpa was going to give me, but instead of getting what I deserved, I got what I didn't deserve— grace. While Grandpa reminded me that your sins will find you out, Grandma reminded me that God's grace and mercy are greater than my sin. I am reminded of the words of Jesus, recorded in Matthew 23:37: "O Jerusalem, Jerusalem, thou that killest the prophets, and stonest them which are sent unto thee, how often would I have gathered thy children together, even as a hen gathereth her chickens under her wings, and ye would not!"

In spite of our faults and failures, Christ calls us to come under the wings of His protection. He seeks to give us not what we deserve, but what we need, God's grace and mercy.

2

A Time of Struggle, Resistance, and Conflict

There was once a man who loved to sit on his front porch every morning and enjoy the fresh air and sunshine of the new day. On one particular morning, he noticed a small cocoon hanging from one of his trees. Each day he would observe the development of the cocoon, the changing color and size. Finally, one morning he noticed that the butterfly inside the cocoon was beginning to break out. The slit in the cocoon was very small, and it seemed that the butterfly was having such a difficult time with it. So the man reached into his pocket and took out a small pen-knife to open the cocoon a little more. This would make it easier for the butterfly to escape. Very soon the butterfly was free of his cocoon and hung by a small thread. Minutes, then hours went by and the butterfly still had not opened his wings to take flight. In fact, the wings never opened and the butterfly never flew. He simply died at that point in his short life.

What the man did not realize was that the butterfly needed the resistance from the cocoon in order to develop strength in its wings, so that when it escaped, it would be able to finish its development. The struggle and resistance were of utmost importance in the development of the butterfly. Without them, he would never achieve his full potential.

Just as God would not take away the struggle and resistance from the butterfly's life, so He will not take it away from our lives. Struggle and resistance are a vital part of the process of coming to our full potential. They were necessary for Jesus, and they are necessary for us.

Therefore, the imperative from Jesus to those who would follow him is that they "take up their cross daily." We bring with us in life our own unique struggles, resistance, and conflict. Jesus did not come into the world to take this away, but instead to share in it. He came to be a part of it, so that we might become all that we were meant to be. Again we are reminded that when these things come upon us, it does not mean that God has forsaken us. In fact, He has drawn even closer to us.

Struggles, resistance and conflicts are a part of life. There is also the pain and suffering that goes along with all of this. Our Lord knows this very well, and invites us to "come unto Him, all who labor and are heavy laden, and He will give us rest." This does not mean that He will take the struggles, resistance, and conflicts away from us, but that He will give Himself to us and will remain Emmanuel, God with us.

The French theologian, Teilhard de Chardin, has said that we are not earthly beings having a spiritual experience, but instead spiritual beings having an earthly experience. The emphasis here is upon the "spiritual" component of our existence. Everything we do in our physical being finds its meaning and value in the spiritual realm.

So the question to ask as we experience struggles, resistance, and conflict in our lives is: "Can I grow as a person from this experience? If so, what is it that I need to give back to my family, community, and nation?' In these questions, we may find meaning and purpose for our lives and a will to go on.

3

A Call in the Night

It was Christmas Eve 2003, and it was my week to be the On Call Chaplain. Six months before, I had arrived in Germany as part of a "Backfill" for the First Armored Division, which was the first unit called into the War in Iraq. Fifty chaplains and chaplain's assistants had been called up by the Army to fill in for the personnel who had been called "down-range" (that is, sent to Iraq).

My unit HQ (headquarters) was located in Giessen, but I was assigned to the Ray Barracks Post in Freiberg, with the title of OIC (Officer in Charge) of the Ray Barracks Chapel. The chaplains assigned to the 323rd Battalion rotated On Call Duty from week to week.

As the Staff Duty Chaplain, I would be called upon by the MPs (Military Police) as needed in cases of domestic violence and other family emergencies. Also, upon notice, I would assist the Staff Duty Officer in providing death notification to family members. The Death Notification Team was composed of one officer and one chaplain. Once the Death Notification Officer had made the announcement to the family, he went back to the car, leaving the chaplain behind to help the family deal with the tragic news.

It was around 7:30 in the evening, and I was in my apartment doing some reading. I had with me three cellphones. One was my personal cell phone, another was for communication to my unit and the third was for emergencies needing my attention as the Staff Duty Chaplain. The Staff Duty cellphone rang, and it was a call from Brigade HQ informing me that there had been a death down-range. The Command Sergeant Major had been killed earlier that day. We needed to notify his wife.

Upon arrival, the Death Notification Officer and I made our way to the apartment. He knocked on the door, and within a few minutes a woman opened the door. The officer asked if she were Mrs. Cook, and the lady nodded.

At the first sight of us, an officer and a chaplain, those who have been associated with the Army for any length of time know what is happening. The officer informed Mrs. Cook that her husband had been killed that day and then went back to the van. It was that quick! Too quick for me!

The news hit Mrs. Cook like a ton of bricks. She ran back into the apartment screaming, "Oh, no, no, no, no!" Fortunately, Mrs. Cook had some family members with her that evening. Her brother came to the door, and I asked if I could come in. I explained to the family who I was and expressed my sorrow that CSM Cook had been killed. I sat next to Mrs. Cook until the friends from the van came in, when I stood up to let one of her friends sit next to her.

There were no details of his death at this time. That would come later. I stood and watched as the family struggled with this most bitter news. My words were few, and came only after I had allowed myself to be exposed to the grief, hurt, and pain of this untimely death. On several occasions, I offered to pray if that would be meaningful for the family, but never got consent from anyone.

After being there for an hour or more, I finally left. Since they were not open to public prayer, I expressed to the family that I would remember them in my prayers, and then I either shook hands or gave each one a hug.

A few weeks later, a memorial service was scheduled for the Ray Barracks Post. In light of the fact that CSM Cook had been the top enlisted person on post, a large crowd was expected, so the service was to take place in the Theater on Post. I wore my Class A uniform that day, and left from the Ray Barracks Chapel thirty minutes prior to the service.

Two lieutenants met me when I arrived at the Post Theater and asked me to come with them. I really did not understand what was going on. At about that time, my chaplain supervisor, LTC Davies, called me aside. It seems that Mrs. Cook did not want to see me at the service. She had informed my superiors that I was the most insensitive man she had ever met in her life, and she wanted nothing to do with me.

LTC Davies said that it would be okay for me to stand at the back of the Theater, but I refused his offer. No, if she did not want me there, then I would leave immediately. I would honor her wishes. I never meant to cause her pain when I went to her home that night, and I certainly did not intend to add insult to injury.

Rejection is hard to take. It eats away at the inner core of whom and what you perceive yourself to be. All sorts of doubts flooded my mind, my soul, my spirit. How in God's name could I have made such a blunder? What else could I have done? The questions came faster than did answers. A feeling of melancholy came over me. The wind had gone from my sails. I was a useless human being. How could I look my fellow chaplains in the eye?

I wish that these feelings and emotions were short lived, but not so. I kept re-playing the tape in my mind, over and over again. In spite of the encouraging words from my peers and supervisors, I still could not let go of all the negative feelings running wild through my mind. I would wake up in the middle of the night, trying to process what had happened that night in the Cooks' home.

I was like an airplane falling out of the sky; I kept going deeper and deeper into depression. I was seemingly unable to pull myself out of the dive. After giving some thought to the issue, I realized it was my family who helped me to turn things around.

My wife and daughter made trips to Germany on separate occasions to see me. Being able to reconnect with my family allowed me to move beyond the rejection I had experienced, and to reinvest my life in those who loved me, warts and all. As I moved in their direction, I moved away from the feelings of rejection and disappointment.

Families are God's gift to us. Healthy families are able to help their members heal and grow. In the Book of Genesis, God says to Adam, "It's not good for man to be alone; I will make a help-meet for you." We heal better in community than we do alone.

Healthy families can give encouragement and acceptance to members who are hurting physically or mentally. They can make us feel wanted and loved. Being attached to a loving and caring family goes a long way in the recovery of soul! The families I speak of do not have to be blood related. Similar familial relationships can come from a class at church or a group from work.

Wherever we experience this phenomenon of family, it is a gift of God. It is His blessing bestowed upon us through a loving and caring fellowship. May God grant you the gift of family as you journey through life and, when you are down, so that you may experience the recovery of your soul.

4

A Cliff Hanger

It seems that a certain hiker, in the mountains of Western North Carolina, was admiring the beautiful fall colors of the leaves as he made his way through the woods. Caught up in this display of nature and not looking where he was going, he fell over the edge of a cliff. Luckily for him, he was able to grab hold of a bush growing from the side of the cliff. Dangling from mid-air over a 200-foot drop, he began to cry out "Help! Help! Is anybody up there? Can anybody hear me?"

To this request came the response "Yes, this is the Lord, and I have heard your cry for help. What do you want?"

The hiker replied, "I need you to get me off this cliff."

The Lord said, "I can do that, just follow my instructions."

"What do you want me to do, the man asked?"

To this the Lord replied, "Just let go."

For a few moments there was silence from the side of the cliff, and then a voice could be heard, "Help! Help! Is there anybody else up there?"

Often, it is the difficult situations of life that allow us to discover a new perspective. That is, the negative experience of life brings enlightenment to the positive side of life. Death ennobles life. Darkness gives appreciation for the light. Hunger brings thankfulness for the pieces of bread. Sickness teaches the meaning of health. These are lessons that we'd rather not experience, but for the most part the decision is not ours to make. Christianity teaches us that life is born out of death, and the meaning of life is often found in suffering and self-sacrifice. Hope is found at the foot of a Cross.

God has placed Himself right in the midst of life where people live and die. Therefore, those who suffer may do one of two things: they may choose to hide behind it, that is, become bitter over it and give up on life altogether, or they may offer it back to God and allow Him to use it for the greater good of humanity. It then becomes our gift to God.

The difficult part of this process is the letting go of our control and trusting God to do the right thing. A song from the 70s by Love Song, "Front Seat, Back Seat Driver" and a more recent version by Carrie Underwood, "Jesus Take the Wheel," reminds us that giving up control of our life is not an easy matter.

Yet, if we want to experience the healing that our Lord seeks to bestow upon us, we need to attempt to align our lives with His. There are two types of wisdom in this world. One is called "conventional wisdom." This is the most popular way of doing business in the world. For example, if a corporation needs to make some cuts to make budget, "conventional wisdom" says to start at the bottom and work up the corporate ladder.

The other type of wisdom is called "Divine Wisdom." This is the less popular way of doing business in the world. It works this way: if a corporation needs to make some cuts to make budget, "Divine Wisdom" starts at the top by taking a look at corporate bonuses and pay incentives at the top of the corporate ladder. "Divine Wisdom" puts the greater sacrifice on those who can better afford it.

This is a Kingdom Principle. It is affirmed by John 3:16, "God loved the world, that He sacrificed His Only Begotten Son, that whosoever believes in Him would have everlasting life." See what I mean! The cut was made at the top, not at the bottom.

God did not say, "I'm going to take the lowest forms of humanity and sacrifice them for the good of the world." No, that's not what He did. He started at the top, not the bottom.

Now, in light of what has been written here, how difficult is it to forego "conventional wisdom" and to embrace "Divine Wisdom?" Look around you! How often do you see "Divine Wisdom" at work in your world? A lot less than "conventional wisdom," I bet.

So, again here is the situation, you are facing a very difficult moment in life. What to do? Do you hold on to what you have, or do you let go and let God take control?

Do you send a kid out to face a giant? Do you take twelve untrained men to head up your company? It's a cliff hanger. What will you do?

5

A Dog's Tail

One morning when my father came in from work, he asked me a question that any eight-year-old boy would love to answer, "Do you want a dog?" My father worked with Mr. Wright on the "Graveyard Shift" at Grace Cotton Mill, located between the towns of Ruth and Rutherfordton, NC. Mr. Wright's Boston terrier had given birth to six puppies, and he had asked my father if I would like to have one of them.

Of course, my answer was an emphatic, "Yes!" So Dad and I went to Mr. Wright's home to get one of the puppies. While I did not know Mr. Wright, I did know his daughter, Nancy, who was also in the second grade at Ruth Elementary School.

Mr. Wright took us around to the side of his house and opened the door to a crawl space under the house. There at the entrance sat the mother Boston terrier with her six puppies. I was the first to choose from this litter, so I looked them over very closely and noticed a puppy at the back. I don't remember what drew my attention to this particular one, but that was the puppy I wanted.

Mr. Wright reached in and picked the puppy up and handed it to me. "You have chosen one of the male puppies," he said to my father and me. That was fine with me, and my dad seemed to be okay with my choice, too.

Sometimes we bring things into our life, not knowing just how they will influence us later on. This was certainly true of Buster, the name my mom gave the dog. Some eight or nine years later, when I was a junior at Fairforest High School in Spartanburg, SC, the dog came up missing. We looked everywhere, but there was no sign of the dog. A week or so went by and still no sign of the dog. It seemed that he was gone for good.

I remember late one evening, going out on the back porch and making a wager with God. My wager was, "God, if You will bring my dog back, I'll join Your church." The challenge was plain and simple. If You do that, I'll do this.

Another week or so went by and still no sign of the dog. We had come to the point of accepting the fact that Buster was not going to be found. Several weeks later on a Friday, I came in from school as usual and there in the middle of the living room floor was Buster. He had been gone for more than three weeks and there he sat, looking as good as the day he left.

It seems that somehow he had gotten into the next door neighbor's basement and couldn't get out. The Staceys had a coal bin in their basement, and somehow Buster must have slid down into the coal bin. It was amazing that after three weeks without food or water, the dog looked so healthy. But he did!

After all the excitement of having Buster back home

again, my thoughts returned to my wager with God on the back porch. "If you bring my dog back, I'll join Your church." I had not said anything about this wager to anyone, but I knew that I had to carry through my promise to God.

The following Sunday, Reverend Terrill at Grace Baptist Church on Whitlock Street poured out his heart and soul in a sermon that I have no remembrance of whatsoever. But that didn't matter; I came forward when the invitation was given to request membership in the church. The following Sunday, I was baptized into God's Church, along with Nonie Lynch, who had come forward the Sunday before as well.

Several years later, while in school at Spartanburg Technical College and struggling with the electronic technology course I was taking, I encountered God's call for me to go into a full-time Christian Vocation. After ten years in the pastorate, over twenty years as chaplain in the Army, and nearly twenty-four years as a hospital chaplain, I'm still learning what that means. It is a dog's tale with a good ending.

6

A Man and His Dog

It was a hot summer day with the humidity as high as a kite. I was sitting in my living room watching a Saturday afternoon baseball game on TV. As I looked out my window, I saw an elderly man and his dog sitting at the edge of my yard. They were apparently taking a break on their journey and decided to stop at my place.

The old man had a hat with a wide brim and a sack of goods he carried on his back. His faithful companion lay still beside him under the hot summer sun. There were some morsels of food that the man shared with his dog, and he then poured some water in a small container for his canine friend.

After some thirty minutes or so, the man and his dog moved on down the road to a destination unknown to me—unknown to me because during this whole interlude that had played out before my eyes, I did not make one effort to make contact with them. There I sat in a house full of food of some sort and water and drinks galore, yet I made no effort to share what I had with these strangers.

For whatever reason, it never entered my mind to turn off the TV and go outside and introduce myself and invite the man and his dog to sit on my front porch with the shade that it would have provided, and to offer them both food and drink. No, I remained there in my cozy little world and did nothing to help them.

How selfish and self-centered can a person get? How indifferent and uncaring can a person be? Well, it certainly was a sad commentary for someone who should have known better.

In the Sermon on the Mount, found in the Gospel according to Matthew, the first Beatitude hits me right between the eyes: "Blessed are the poor in spirit, for theirs is the Kingdom of Heaven." A popular way of understanding this saying is that Jesus is speaking of those who have realized how spiritually poor they are. The problem here is that the Hebrew mindset did not divide human beings into body and spirit.

The Book of Genesis informs us that God created human beings as living souls. The soul then is not just a part of a human being, but includes the entire person —mind, body, and spirit. So to talk about one is to talk about the other two as well.

We are blessed when we are poor in spirit, because such is the character of God, and the person of Jesus. In creation God held nothing back, but gave His very best and upon inspection of what He had brought into existence, said that it was good, very good.

One of the things that Jesus did as he walked upon this earth was to show us what a God-filled human life looked like. He was our model for what it means to be human. He had compassion for those he met who were in need. He did not look the other way or pretend they weren't there. When you spent time in Jesus' presence, you got his very best.

To be "poor in spirit" means that we are willing to give our very best to those around us in need. It means that we have compassion for those who are struggling with life and that we offer to them our best. The lady in Phil Collins' song "Another Day in Paradise" felt like she was transparent because no one noticed her. No one acknowledged that she even existed. They walked around her, too busy to get involved.

That was my problem that hot summer day that God sent a man and his dog my way. I was too full of myself to give my best to these two. I was too caught up in my world to give my best to their world. Whatever was going on with me that day, I was not "poor in Spirit." I was unable or unwilling to give my best to a fellow human being in need. It was a golden opportunity to draw near to God; to draw near to our Lord, but I would not. The Good News is that God has given me many new opportunities to be "poor in spirit."

7

A Near Death Experience

One summer when I was around five years old, my parents and grandparents decided to go visit some of our relatives up in the mountains of Western North Carolina. I have no idea how we got there, but at some point we parked the car and started walking down a narrow pathway into the woods. Eventually we came to a clearing in the woods, and there it was—a log cabin! We found our relatives sitting under a large oak tree.

They showed us around the place and eventually took us to a barn not too far away. The trip to the barn was along a narrow pathway on a hillside. On the way back, I was running ahead of everyone along this narrow pathway when one of the dogs passed me and caused me to lose my balance. I began to roll down the hillside until I finally hit a small tree. In fact, I hit the tree in the center of my small body, which knocked the breath out of me.

My Uncle Furman made the trip down the hillside to help me back up to the path. I did not know the danger that I was in until one of our relatives pointed beyond the small tree to a cliff. He said the cliff dropped off for about 200 feet into a rocky river-bottom, and I would not have survived the fall. Also, he noted the tree I landed up against was the last tree before the cliff.

I have always been thankful for the small tree that got in my way on that hillside. It literally saved my life. In fact there have been a number of things that have gotten in my way throughout my life. Looking back, I must say, I thank God for the intrusions that have been blessings in disguise.

The writer of Ecclesiastes says that, "to everything there is a season, and a time to every purpose under the heaven." Sometimes the things we consider to be a hindrance to our hopes, dreams, and goals in life may in fact be more of a blessing than a curse. We do not always know what God is up to with us. We walk by faith, not by sight. We are called upon to trust in God's on-going activity in our journey of life.

We become distraught and angry when a relationship doesn't work out: we don't get the promotion; we apply for a job and it goes to someone else; we want to go to a certain school, but things get in our way and we end up somewhere else.

I believe that God is never leading us down a dead-end street and that, from time to time, He allows things to get in our way so that we might be in His way.

8

A Ride That Won't Let Go

We had been to the Cleveland County Fair more times than I could count, but this time would be different. While my wife and I were not interested in the rides, our four-year-old daughter wanted to ride everything. After a few trips around the fairgrounds, she decided that she wanted to go through the Fun House.

I decided not to go along, but instead observe from the outside as they went through and around various obstacles. One particular obstacle that was clearly visible from the outside was the "round barrel," which continually turned at a very slow pace. From one end of the barrel to the other was about five or six feet. No problem for our daughter! She was in and through this obstacle in a blink of an eye, but not so for my wife.

Somewhere between the going in and the getting out, she fell down. The next series of events were like a slow motion movie. Each time my wife would almost make it upright, the slow turning barrel would cause her to lose her balance again and down she would go. I can't count the number of times she repeated this process. The crowd that was gathering outside watching this spectacle was pulling for her, too, but only to be disappointed time and time again.

Well, I believe that we would still be there today if it were not for this hand that came from nowhere and pulled her to safety. Those assembled outside the Fun House cheered loudly when the lady in distress had been rescued.

The scriptures over and over again emphasize that we all are in the hands of God. In his letter to the Romans, Paul reminds his audience that nothing can snatch them from the hands of God, that neither things present, nor things past, nor things yet to come can separate them from God's loving embrace in Christ Jesus.

From the Sea of Galilee comes the story of Jesus and His disciples, who were in a boat far from land. In the early morning hours, Jesus came to them walking on the water. Peter asked to join Him and was given permission. On his way to Jesus, Peter got distracted by the storm and began to sink. He called out to be rescued, whereupon, Jesus reached out and pulled him to safety.

Today the unseen hands of God are still active in our lives. The hands that brought Creation into being are the same hands that continue to mold and form us into the human beings we were meant to be. Yes, we all are in God's hands, and that's not a bad place to be.

9

A Song, a Touch and a Prayer

It was the finest medical center in the country. People from all over the world came here to find treatment and healing for their diseases. This facility had the best doctors, best equipment, and best staff of any hospital in the country.

Within this hospital, there were several cancer units that had similar patients. When an overview of the patients' records from the various units was compiled, it was discovered that one of the units was consistently doing much better than the other units. On this particular unit, patients were discharged in a shorter time frame. They also used less pain medication than those in the other units, and their overall approval rating was much higher.

These results puzzled the medical staff. Why was this particular unit doing so much better than the others? What was going on in that unit that was not happening in the other units? Since all the units had the same medical staff and nursing staff, and same treatment plan, there was no easy answer. The records were checked and re-checked to determine if the staff had made an error, but no errors were found. The difference remained a mystery, until late one night.

On this particular night, one of the medical staff was making his rounds on a late schedule. As the doctor went from room to room, he noticed that the cleaning lady was softly humming and singing a song that would later be identified as "God Will Take Care of You." In addition to singing this song very softly, she would gently touch each patient and whisper "God will take care of you."

Further investigation revealed that this cleaning lady was assigned to this particular unit. Each night as she made her rounds, she sang this hymn, touched and spoke to each patient. A song, a touch and a prayer were the difference.

Who would have ever thought that a song, a touch, and a prayer would make all that difference? But it did. In spite of the hospital's having one of the best pastoral care departments in the country, it was a cleaning lady who brought the healing presence of God to the patients in that unit.

I find a bit of humor in the fact that the medical, nursing and pastoral staffs could not put these patients back together again, but the cleaning lady could. She was the one chosen by God to extend His presence to these cancer patients. Not that the other staff members were not important, but the cleaning lady added a dimension that had been missing in the care of these patients. While she was going about her usual duties, she took the time to be present through a song, a touch and a prayer.

Part of the mystery of God is that He accomplishes His work through a variety of people. Some folks get the idea that only ordained clergy can fill this role, but that's not the case. The New Testament has numerous references to the fact that we are a kingdom of priests. We all have been ordained by God to carry His Good News into the world.

So as we travel through this world, doing whatever we have been called to do, be aware that we are channels of God's healing presence. God seems to choose some of the most unlikely folks to spread the Good News. Post Resurrection Day, it was a woman, some think Mary Magdalene, who was the first to proclaim the Good News. It is an unlikely choice for many, but not for our Lord.

If a song, a touch and a prayer can make so much difference, think of the ways as you journey through life that you, too, can make a difference. Remember, with God all things are possible.

10

A Trip to the Beach

We had been planning the trip for some time. My daughter, Lauran and her family would be joining us on this trip to the beach, along with our granddaughter, Taylor. We looked forward to getting away from our busy work schedules and having some time to kick back and relax.

Upon arrival, we found the weather to be perfect. There was hardly a cloud in the sky, and a gentle breeze was blowing in from the ocean. We set up camp under a large umbrella with lounge chairs. As I took my place in one of the chairs, I leaned back and thought to myself, "It just doesn't get any better than this."

My wife always brings enough sunscreen lotion to sink a battleship. She is constantly monitoring each family member to ensure that we have enough of this stuff all over our bodies. I did not plan to get out into the sun that day, so I declined her offer. I had brought several books I wanted to read, and this seemed the perfect time to do so.

I don't remember how many hours we spent on the beach,

but by the end of the day we all were ready to get back to our apartment. There are some things that you do not notice while at the beach, such as just how much sun you are getting. Back at the apartment, I discovered that I was red as a tomato. Although I had been out in the sun only for a short time, I had received wind burns.

My wife and I, plus our granddaughter, made a trip to the local drugstore. As the clerk was showing us where all the good anti-sunburn stuff was located, our granddaughter, walking behind us, kept calling out, "He did it to himself." One time would have been enough, but not for our granddaughter, who kept up the chant, "He did it to himself," over and over again.

What I disliked about her words the most was that they were true. I was suffering because I had refused to put sunscreen lotion on, and now I was paying the price for my bad decision. My wife had offered to help me get the lotion on my back, but I refused her offer. Like the sermon by R.G. Lee, "Payday Someday," that someday was a lot sooner than I had wished.

The scriptures tell us that we will "reap what we sow." God grants us freedom of choice. He does not try to manipulate or coerce us into doing anything. He allows us the freedom to choose for ourselves. At the end of the day, we have no one to blame but ourselves.

He offers us forgiveness of the wrong we have committed. His desire is not for punishment or revenge, but healing. There is a beautiful scripture passage found in Matthew 23:37, where Jesus speaks of the healing that he wanted to provide: "O Jerusalem, Jerusalem, the one who continues to destroy yourself and others! I have sent my messengers to you, but you will not listen. How often I wanted to gather you to myself, as a hen gathers her chicks under her wings, but you were not willing!" (The paraphrasing is mine.)

All we have to do is just put our name in the place of "Jerusalem," and know that God calls out to each of us in the midst of our hurt and pain.

11

A Tug of War with the Dentist

At the tender age of ten, I came down with a bad toothache. At this time in my short life all the baby teeth were gone, so this was a permanent tooth that was causing me so much discomfort. In previous times, my dad would tie a string around my baby tooth, give it a quick jerk and out it would come. But since this was a permanent tooth with deeper roots, the decision was made to take me to the dentist. Normally, it was my mom who would take me, but for some reason, which I can't remember, the task was turned over to my dad.

At the dentist's office the doctor took a look and determined that the tooth needed to be pulled. So, of course, this was not good news for me. Since this was my first trip to the dentist's office, there was some concern on my part as to what would happen next.

Well, I didn't have to wait long to find out. Very soon the dentist came back with a needle and injected some stuff in my gums. He told my dad that it would take a few minutes for that side of my mouth to become numb. Several minutes went by and eventually the dentist came back with a tool that looked like a pair of pliers. He asked me to open my mouth wide and began to pull on a tooth on the other side of my mouth. This hurt! With his hand in my mouth, it was impossible for me to tell the man that he was trying to pull the wrong tooth.

So, my only option under the circumstances was to bite him, which I did. It worked! Immediately he pulled his hand from my mouth and said what I considered a bad word. This sort of word was not new to me, in that I had heard my father use it quite often. So, I shared with him some of the bad words that I had added to my vocabulary. Being quite taken back by my ability to use words not allowed to be named here, he told me he was going to call the police. Once again, I reached into my bag of dirty words and told him what he could do with the police.

Unfortunately, by the time my dad stepped in to calm me down, the damage had been done. I can't remember if I got a spanking when I got home, but certainly I deserved one. It was not the best of days for me or for the dentist. That was not our best behavior, but sometimes in life we say and do things that are not good for us or for others. I have since learned that saying "I'm sorry" is a good way to deal with these unfortunate events in life.

On the T.V. show "Happy Days," the Fonz could not say the words, "I'm sorry." We ought not to be like the Fonz, but more like the One who said, "You have heard it said of old, an eye for an eye, and a tooth for a tooth...but I say unto you forgive others that have wronged you, as your heavenly Father has forgiven you."

Life lived without forgiveness is a life filled with resentment, which can be defined as the perception that we have been treated unfairly. If resentment is left unattended, it may develop into hatred and hatred into some form of action against the person who treated us unjustly. The ill feelings become a vicious cycle that never ends, much like the Hatfield and McCoy families who carried on their feud after the Civil War.

The scripture warns us not to let the sun go down on our anger, because it can cause a lot more pain and suffering for us and others. There are some things that we need to let go of in life, and grudges would be one of those things.

May God grant all of us the desire and ability to let go of our hurt and pain in order to allow God's forgiveness to fully embrace our lives.

12

Am I My Brother's Keeper?

We lived in the smallest house in the Grace Cotton Mill Village, located between the beautiful communities of Ruth and Rutherfordton, NC. Next to our home was a patch of woods with a path going into it. All the kids who went to Ruth Elementary School from the mill village used this path. As the crow flies, the distance from the mill village to the school was about a mile.

On a number of occasions, I asked my mom where all the kids were going, and she told me that they were going to school. So one morning, when mom wasn't looking, I got a notepad and a pencil, fell at the back of the pack and off to school I went.

Since I was but four years of age, it was quite evident that I did not belong to this group. How far I went down the pathway with them I don't remember, but two girls in the group noticed me and escorted me back to my parents' home. It just so happened they knew where I belonged and took the time to get me back home safe and sound.

I wonder! I wonder! What if none of the kids had noticed me? What if no one had taken the time to get me back home? What would have happened to me? I'm sure that a four-year-old could not have kept pace with a group of kids much older. Somewhere along the way, I would have gotten lost. Maybe I would have fallen into the small creek, that in some places was deep enough for a child my size to drown.

I don't know if the girls who took the time to take me back home were late for school that day or not. I don't even know who they were, but I do know what they did for me and for my parents. Maybe they saved my life, or at least saved me from a very bad experience.

"Am I my brother's keeper?" is the question that came from Cain. He was approached by God concerning what had happened to his brother. Cain's response is more of a statement than it is a question. The implication is, "No, it's not my day to look after him."

There was a day when that question would have been answered with an affirmative "Yes." In days gone by, neighbor looked after neighbor, because there was a sense of responsibility and duty to help in a time of need. I remember spending some time on my grandparents' farm in Polk County, Nc. One of the neighbors needed a new roof on his barn. It seems that the men in the community got together and put the new barn roof on in one day. No one was paid! It was what any decent neighbor would do for another neighbor.

The story of the "Good Samaritan," found in Luke 10:30–36, addresses the issue of how we are related to the world. In this story, there are a number of issues that impact the response of the priest, the Levite, and the Samaritan. There is the religious issue of coming into contact with a person considered to be unclean. There is the issue of personal safety and the risk of stopping in that part of the country to help someone. There is the socio-economic issue of "What will this cost me, if I stop to help this person?" The big difference between the priest, the Levite, and the Samaritan is that the Samaritan had "compassion" for the person on the side of the road. Compassion is the trump card. Compassion overcomes the restraints of religious, personal, and social issues in order to do the right thing.

Am I my brother's keeper? A tough choice in a busy world! May God grant unto us the compassion to say, "Yes."

13

Bad Things Happen

There is a story about a man who had it all. He was wealthy beyond belief. No one in the state of Texas had anything on him. He owned more land and cattle than anyone else, and of course, he had more money than anyone else. He was at the top of his profession. No one could come anywhere close to having all the power and influence he had throughout the land. All political leaders sought his advice on matters pertaining to national and international affairs.

The man also had a very large family with twelve children, six boys and six girls. His wife was very attractive and active in the local community. You name it and this family had it.

Sometimes when people have so much, they tend to forget about God because they are so busy, but not this man. He maintained a very good relationship with God. He was an honest man and did not cheat anyone, but was fair to all who did business with him.

Although he was not a perfect man, he was a good husband,

father, and neighbor. He did not ask of someone else what he wouldn't do himself. He was an excellent model of modesty and was always true to his word. It was often said of him that a handshake and his word were all you needed to seal a deal.

As in all our lives, there come days of cloudy weather. Dark clouds form and the wind blows, and the rains come until . . . lightening hits and then . . . a house bursts into flames and twelve children die. It was the worst news any parent could receive. Some of the most beautiful children in the world, and now they were all gone.

Not long after this, a disease killed nearly all his cattle in a matter of a few weeks. His prize bulls all gone! In spite of receiving the best of care, the cattle were no match for this horrible disease.

No one is sure, but most likely the stress of losing all the children and the other events on the ranch had caused his wife to develop some serious health problems, and she soon died.

As if that were not enough to deal with, the man himself came down with some health problems. He had developed sores all over his body, which put him in great misery and pain. All alone, and without any support system, he felt disconnected from the world. But fortunately for him, he had friends to come see him in his hour of need.

As his friends sat there with him in the living room, they did so in complete silence. Not a word was spoken, just complete silence! Finally, a week rolled by, and then one of his friends spoke up and asked the question that was on everybody's mind:

"My friend, what have you done to cause God to do this to you?"

The man had no answer. He had no idea why all the bad things were happening to him and his family. He believed deep down in his soul that he had done nothing wrong to deserve this sort of treatment.

On numerous occasions, he had approached God with questions about why all these things were happening to him. Over and over he agonized about why all these things were happening, but in the end, he never received an answer.

His friends came from the old school, and believed that if you were having problems, you had committed some kind of sin. Essentially, they thought that people who suffer have done something wrong to deserve it. Innocent people don't suffer!

Others in his group suggested that he curse God and then commit suicide. He stood fast. He believed that God had not forsaken him or his family and ranch. He was willing to live with the questions unanswered.

Maybe someday, the answers would come to him, but maybe not. Either way, he would remain true to his God. In his darkest hour, he was aware of the presence of God, and how close God had drawn to him.

We aren't promised to have all the answers in life, but we are promised that our Lord will not forsake us or leave us in our darkest hour. Live with the questions. Unanswered questions allow us to encounter the mystery of God. He is always at work in mysterious ways in each and every life. He is at work in our unanswered questions.

Bad things happen, that's for sure. But God's purpose and will for our life is never destroyed by bad things. Out of the rubble of every life, He is able to bring forth that which has meaning and purpose.

The "Cross" is a symbol of the worst that could be done to God, yet even the "Cross" did not overcome God's creative power to re-create and make all things new. When bad things happen, God creates new possibilities!

14

Behind Closed Doors

Here we go again, another trip to the mountains to see some of our relatives. We had been to this place before, so I knew what to expect. The log cabin was set out in an open area on top of one of the Blue Ridge Mountains in Western North Carolina. There certainly were some very beautiful views of the world from up there.

On previous visits, we had been allowed to enter the cabin. The floor was covered in wood planks, and some of it was still just dirt. In the kitchen, there was a wood stove and a back window from which a cord ran down the mountain side into an artesian well. The bucket on this cord would bring back some of the coldest water you would ever want to drink.

The cabin was lit by candlelight and heated by a large fireplace that functioned as a stove as well. The toilet was located about a hundred feet or so down the mountain side.

Everything seemed normal when we arrived on this trip. As usual, we had to walk about a hundred feet from where our car was parked through a small patch of woods to the open clearing where the cabin was located.

In the summer months our relatives spent a lot of time outside the cabin under a very large oak tree, and this is where we found them on that particular day. I am not sure how long we had been there when a storm came up. Uncle Marick, as he was called, collected his family and went into the cabin, leaving the rest of us outside in the storm.

For some reason we were not allowed into the cabin on this particular visit. On the trip back home, my parents and my father's parents discussed this strange occurrence. I don't believe that anyone came up with an answer for what had happened up there on the mountain.

As I look back, I see this was quite a different approach from my grandparents on my mother's side of the family. Staying with them one summer, I remember when we all went to town on Saturday mornings, they would leave a note on the front door that read: "Gone to town! We'll be back soon. Come on in and make yourself at home!"

That was back in the days when doors were left unlocked. Not so today. In my neighborhood, most of the homes have a sign out front to warn the general public that they are wired against intruders.

On a personal note, we must all decide whom we let into our life and whom we keep out. I have been hurt by some folks I have let into my life, while others have been a great blessing to me. Sometimes it is difficult to know whom to let in and whom to keep out.

In the Book of Revelation 3:20, we have these words of Jesus concerning a closed door: "Here I Am! I stand at the door and knock. If you hear me knocking and open the door, I will come in and we will have Communion together."

Jesus is not like the big, bad wolf that huffs and puffs until he blows your door open. Nor will He bypass your door and come down your chimney while you are asleep. No, He uses the direct approach. You must be willing to open your door and invite Him in.

15

Bumps, Bruises, and Bicycles

I can remember that day like it was yesterday. That is, the day my parents bought me my first bicycle, a bright red bike just the right size for a six-year-old. Now all I had to do was learn how to ride it.

Fortunately for me, my cousin Evelyn also wanted to learn how to ride a bike. I held the bike for her, and she held it for me. With a good push, we could ride as far as our momentum would take us. That old bike must have been a good one, for it certainly endured a lot of abuse that day.

After many falls and as many bruises, we both learned how to ride the bike. That is not to say we never fell again, for we did from time to time. Usually, we had no one and nothing to blame for our wrecks other than our own carelessness.

Life is full of bumps and bruises. We all have our ups and downs. The Gospel Accounts are full of episodes in which

Jesus challenged those that had experienced some of life's bumps and bruises to get up and go on with their lives. This invitation was extended to a variety of people, in a variety of life situations.

It has been rightly observed that our greatest achievement in life is not that we never fall down or never make a mistake, but that every time we do, we get back up and try again and again and again. Jesus reminds us that His healing presence will be with us and because He is active in all aspects of our lives, it is possible for us to overcome our bumps and bruises.

16

Cauthman's Cat

The cafeteria at seminary provided decent meals at a good price, but it was not like home cooking. So, when the opportunity presented itself to have a meal in the home of one of my classmates, it was a real treat. Wofford Cauthman and Cathy Bailey had gotten married during his first year at seminary and rented a home not far from the seminary campus. On a number of occasions they invited me over for dinner, and I never turned down the offer.

On one of my visits to their home, I discovered that they had a new addition to the family, a stray cat that had decided to call their place home. On subsequent visits, Wofford would show us the tricks he had taught the cat. Not a bad performance by a stray cat!

One day at school, Wofford informed me that the cat had been hit by a car and they had taken it to the vet. The injuries were too severe, and the cat died. My response to Wofford was that he could easily get another cat. Why, cats were a dime a dozen, and it should be no problem to find another.

Wofford was deeply hurt by the cat's death, but I was unable to show him any compassion or sympathy. I acted like the cat was yesterday's newspaper, so I just could not understand all this grief. No, at that time I was unable to walk in Wofford's moccasins.

Years later while living in Western North Carolina, my wife and I were the recipients of several stray cats that found their way to our front door. Unfortunately, each cat was stricken with feline leukemia and had to be put to sleep at the vet's office. I took the first one myself, but soon discovered that, like my friend Wofford, I had become very attached to each cat.

It was a heart-wrenching time for me, and I felt, in addition to the grief, a deep regret about how I had responded to Wofford when he had lost his cat. Life had taught me a lesson. I have since learned that our bodies do not distinguish between our grief for a human being and our grief for one of our pets. As far as our bodies are concerned, grief is grief.

I am reminded that the shortest verse in the Bible is found in John 11:35 "Jesus wept." The message here is that we need to be in touch with our emotions. We need to allow ourselves to freely give expression to the emotion we are feeling. If we do not do this, then over a period of time we can build up residual grief.

God made us the way we are, with the capacity to express our emotions, which allows us to heal. There is a saying that "time heals all wounds." That is not true. Time has nothing to do with healing. We heal by allowing our emotions to come to the surface and allowing our tears to flow down our face. Jesus wept! So can we!

17

Choosing Sides

Growing up as an only child in Grace Mill Village, located between the big cities of Ruth and Rutherfordton, NC, was not too bad. Although I did not have brothers and sisters to play with, there was a whole village full of kids. One of our favorite places to play during the summer was down in the old cow pasture. The two oldest kids got to choose sides for the baseball teams. A flip of a coin decided who went first. Of course, each side wanted the best players, so the other big kids went first. Then it came down to me, the question being: Which team had to take me, the smallest, weakest, slowest player in the entire Mill Village? I was seen more as a liability than an asset. Here we go again, another flip of the coin to determine which team had to take me.

The reason that one of the teams had to choose me was that the baseball and bat belonged to me. If I were not chosen by somebody, then I would take my baseball and bat and go home. That was my ace in the hole. It really did not bother me that neither side wanted me, because the important thing to me was that I got to play.

Rejection is never easy to take. Whether it is a job we are seeking, or a relationship with another person, the feeling of not being wanted eats away at our self-esteem and self-confidence. We all have this need to be wanted and accepted. When this doesn't happen, we may end up with some serious self-image problems.

These are not the sort of things that go away with age; we take them with us into adulthood.

With this in mind, the sort of people whom Jesus hung out with should come as no surprise. They were folks no one wanted to be around. They were the outcasts of society. They were people such as tax collectors, prostitutes, and people from the other side of the tracks. There was no place for them at the worship center or any other place in the community. Some were beggars who were sick with an assortment of mental health problems. They were considered to be damaged goods.

But to these folks, Jesus brought Good News. While they were not accepted or wanted within their communities, Jesus accepted them and invited them into His life and ministry. What the world was willing to throw away, God wanted. What the world saw as a hopeless group of people, God saw potential for His kingdom work.

In Matthew 5:3, Jesus says that "Blessed are the weak in spirit, for theirs is the kingdom of heaven."

And in First Corinthians 1:27, the Apostle Paul says that "God chose what the world considered weak to defeat the strong."

Both of these scripture passages make clear that those who are written off by the world as being of no value or importance, God has chosen for His team. He will take and do great things with them. The Good News is you have been chosen. You are accepted and wanted for God's team.

18

Comfort, Comfort My People

We often hear folks talking about the "good old days" and their desire to return to that day and time. I'm not so sure if many of us would be willing to give up all the comforts of today for the more difficult way of life of yesteryear. We have been spoiled a bit by all the modern conveniences. The success of advertising is based on the offer of an easier and better life. Therefore, when we hear the word "comfort," we often think of a warm, contented feeling.

The Scriptures make several promises of comfort. The words from Isaiah are, "Comfort, comfort my people," which became the mission of Isaiah to a people going through a very difficult time. The words of Jesus to his followers were, "I will pray to the Father, and He shall give you another Comforter." These words might cause some to think that the call of God is a call to a life of smooth sailing. In the Old Testament, Job's friends wondered what he had done wrong for God to punish him so much. That thought is still with us today.

In the Bayeux Tapestry in France, there is a section in which King Harold is depicted riding into battle carrying a lance. As he prods his troops with this lance, the caption reads, "King Harold comforts his troops." In the 17th century to comfort someone meant to goad, a means of prodding reluctant servants or animals into action.

So the Comforter (the Holy Spirit) was not being defined as the bearer of peace and tranquility in the absence of Jesus, but as a disturbing, insistent spur, pressing the disciples into action. Our call to come and be followers of Christ is not to a life of smooth sailing, but to a life that is open to the direction of God. In his book, *The Cost of Discipleship*, Dietrich Bonhoeffer writes, "When Christ calls a man (anyone), He bids him come and die."

The old hymn, "Onward Christian Soldiers" reminds us that there is a war going on, and we are engaged in combat. Although at times we may feel alone in this war, the promise is that God is before us and He challenges us as we face the troubled times of life with the assurance that He is active and present in all of our life events. His promise to us is "I'll never leave or forsake you under any circumstance."

19

Dragons, Giants, and Castles

There was once a prince who lived in a castle. The castle was surrounded by a deep body of water and had a large drawbridge. Although there were a lot of beautiful things to see and do outside, the prince would never leave the castle. He had heard about the huge dragon that lived out there somewhere and was afraid of it. So, day after day, he remained in his castle, protected by the high walls and the water that surrounded it.

One day the prince decided that he would venture outside the castle walls and take his chances. He decided that he would rather die a free man than die a prisoner in his own castle. So he ordered that the drawbridge be lowered, walked across it and looked down the hill. Sure enough, there was the dragon, standing there bigger than life.

The prince decided to get it over with, so he started walking toward the dragon, step by step. When he reached the dragon, he stood there and then bent down and picked the dragon up in the palm of his hand. A strange thing had happened as he made his way to the dragon. With each step he took in the direction of the dragon, the fearsome monster had gotten smaller and smaller.

The prince was somewhat angry with himself as he looked at the size of the dragon close up. He said: "I can't believe that I have wasted my life away inside a castle because of you. All these years that I could have been enjoying my life, I have wasted."

To this the dragon responded, "It hasn't been a total waste, because if it were not for me, you would never have known that you could go up against a dragon and win."

In the Old Testament, there is a story of a mighty general and his troops who see a giant across the battlefield and are afraid to go out to encounter him. Along comes a small lad, who picks up a few river rocks, throws his slingshot across his shoulders and goes out to meet this giant of a man. Although the odds are against him, he defeats the giant, who represents opposition to God's will and purpose for His people.

The Apostle Paul writing to the Christians in Rome reminded them that, "If God be for us, who can be against us" (Romans 8:31). Therefore, we can go up against dragons and giants because God is with us. In this we are made aware that we are at all times dependent upon God for strength to confront each day's challenges.

If we are to live life to the fullest, we must be willing to confront the dragons and giants that we find in our own lives. We may choose to run away from them, deny them, or confront them. The way we confront them is to acknowledge that they exist in our lives, and that we fear facing up to them.

The Book of Isaiah 40:31 reads: "They that wait upon the Lord will renew their strength; they will soar on wings like eagles; they will run and not grow weary; they will walk and not be overcome by the challenge before them."

The Lord provides strength and endurance to His people to face the challenges of life. This does not mean that we win all the time, but it does give assurance that even in our defeats, God's strength is available and His grace will be sufficient to sustain us through the turbulent times of life.

20

Dreams of Success

In the majestic foothills of Western North Carolina, there lies a small town off the beaten path. When my wife and I were married, she still had one more year of college to finish, so we moved into Varsity Squire Apartments, located just down the street from Gardner-Webb University.

During our time in Boiling Springs, we both started going to the same hairdresser in the big town of Shelby. Over time we had built a fairly decent friendship with Steve, so on one occasion, he asked us to attend a meeting with him. It seems he was a member of some group that met on a regular basis to inspire people to be better people. Although he did not give much detail about the meeting, he said our attendance would help him meet some of his commitments to the group. It sounded good, so we agreed to attend.

At the meeting we heard a number of testimonies from members of the group on what they were going to do when they made it to the top of the organization. Some were going to send missionaries to various parts of the world, while others were going to use their money on local charities. It seemed that they really had their heart in the right place.

Sitting there, I began to wonder, what are they going to do with what they have now? Are they going to wait until all this money comes rolling in before they start doing something in the present moment? It seemed that they were going to wait until they struck it rich before attempting to do all these noble things they spoke about.

Yes, a person can have dreams of what they will do when this or that happens in life. Yes, when that happens, they will break open their money purses and pour the money out on church and community. Their battle cry is: "Just wait and see what I'm going to do; just you wait!"

Perhaps others will wait for a more opportune time when it is more convenient. Still others will wait for a grander moment when the need is at its highest level and, at that point, will merit the gift that will be provided. Unfortunately, I don't believe that day ever comes. The right time is always somewhere out there in the future, but never in the present moment. I have paraphrased the story from Matthew 26:6-11 to illustrate this point:

One day Jesus was in the town of Bethany at the home of Simon the Leper, a woman came to Him having an alabaster flask of very costly fragrant oil, and she poured it on His head as He sat at the table.

But when His disciples saw it, they were indignant, saying, "Why this waste? For this fragrant oil might have been sold for a lot of money, and given to the poor."

But Jesus defended her actions, saying, "She has done a good work for Me."

The above scripture gives us a view of two paths that can be taken in our journey in life. One view is that of keeping what you have until the right moment comes along. This view fulfills the promise that those that keep their life will lose out on a lot of opportunities to receive a blessing. The second view is that of a person who sees an opportunity to do good with what they have, and they do it. In- stead of keeping life, they seek at every opportunity to give it away.

In the giving of life, wherever it is invested, there are abundant returns. You can't out-give the Lord. All that He has is ours! All that we have is His! There is no limit to His ability to supply what we need, but not necessarily what we want. In this, we discover that the Lord is able to make our dreams come true, not like the illusion at Disney World, but in our everyday world.

In giving our life away, we are drawn closer to our Lord who gave His life for us. This is what true success is all about, not that we hoard up our life, but that we discover ways in which to share it with the world around us.

The Prophet Joel writes that: "The day shall come when God pours out His Spirit upon His people. At this time sons and daughters will proclaim the Good News of God's gift, and the adults will dream dreams of a better world for all humanity." (Joel 2: 28). (My paraphrase.)

21

Going to Nineveh

Once upon a time, there lived a young man in a medium-sized southern town. As he neared the end of his high school education, he had no idea what he wanted to do with his life. Some of his friends were planning to attend a local technical college in the fall, so he decided to do that as well. He took a placement test and scored high enough to take one of the most advanced courses available. He would become an electronic engineer. At the midpoint in his course of study, the young man realized that he had made a mistake. His current endeavor did not seem right for him. One night while lying in bed, he began to wrestle with how uncomfortable he was with the direction his life was going at the time. While feeling rather desperate to find another course of action, he decided to see what the Lord could or would do about his situation. His prayer was simple, "God there must be something else I can do with my life. Help me to find it."

The next thought that came to mind was not the answer he was looking for. If it was from the Lord, it was telling him to prepare for a vocation in bringing Good News to God's people. That sounded simple enough, but the young man was not ready to embrace that calling for his life.

After receiving his degree from the technical college, he got on the first plane to Nineveh. That is, he went out and joined the Air Force. A number of his friends were also doing this at the same time. For him, the way you deal with an issue like this was to run away from it and, hopefully, the issue would go away. It didn't happen!

Upon his return from Nineveh, the call upon his life was renewed to the point that he had to do something. His defense to the Lord was this, "I don't know anything about what You are asking me to do, and so far as I know, I would be hard pressed to find a college that would accept me." (Some of his protest came from the fact that he had nearly flunked out of the technical college and that he had to take Physical Education as a senior in high school in order to graduate.)

"Also, he continued, "it is difficult for me to stand up before a crowd of people and say anything. Just look at my track record from high school."

He would do anything to get out of doing an oral book report. He would make himself sick and ask the principal to let him go home. It became such a problem that eventually the principal informed him the next time he showed up in his office that he (the principal) would give him something to go home about. He knew what that meant and never showed up in the principal's office again. He thought, "Lord, You have called one of the most introverted persons in the world and I can't see myself ever being able to fulfill Your calling for my life."

Still the Lord was persistent in His calling and would not go away. So, just to prove to the Lord that He was wrong this one time, the young man went and took an SAT exam one Saturday morning. Without any sort of reviewing or studying, he knew that his scores would not be good enough to get him into college.

Several weeks went by and finally the scores from the SAT arrived. His score was somewhere between 1100 and 1200, and not really knowing what that meant, he sent his application to Spartanburg Methodist Junior College. To his surprise, a letter of acceptance came back!

Doing everything he could to get out of going in this direction with his life, he now found all the obstacles that he had put in place torn down and destroyed. The Lord was relentless! Apparently, He would not take "no" for an answer.

This young man was not the first to put up such a resistance to the Lord's call. The Old Testament reports two occasions in which this happened. Upon receiving such a call, Isaiah had the following response, my paraphrasing of Isaiah 6:6-8:

"God have mercy on me, for I am not a finished product! I am a man who has said things that I wish I had not said, and I have been greatly influenced by the people around me...."

Then a voice was heard, "I have touched your lips, your sins have been taken away. You are a clean man now..."

Soon after this, I heard a voice saying, "Whom shall I send? And who will go for Me?"

Then I said, "Here I am Lord! Send me!"

When Jeremiah was approached about this matter of calling, his response was as follows: "Ah, Lord God! Can't You see that I cannot speak, for I am so young?"

The Lord's reply was: "It doesn't matter how old you are. What really matters is that I have called you, and those whom I call I will use as I see fit. Because (again my paraphrasing from Jeremiah 1:4-9) before I formed you in the womb of your mother, I knew you; before you were born, I set you aside for My special purpose; I ordained you as a spokesperson to all the nations. I have put My words in your mouth."

In spite of more than thirty years of seeking to fulfill the Lord's call upon my life, I still go through periods of time in which I feel a sense of fear, uncertainty, and doubt about my ability to do what the Lord has called me to do. He continues to surprise me with what He is able to do with me. Personally, I would not have called me to do this work for the Lord, but He was able to see in me what I could not see in myself, and to do with me what is above and beyond my wildest expectations.

The Good News is what our Lord has done with me, and He can do with you. Our full potential is not dependent upon our perceived abilities alone, but upon God's ability to use whatever we submit to Him. God calls us to be open to His will and purpose for our lives. Answering the call is trusting God to lead and equip us to do that which He calls us to.

While, like me, you may choose to go to Nineveh, The Hound of Heaven will pursue until you stop running. Then He will embrace you and take you by the hand and lead you to the place where He wants you to be.

22

Growing Pains

It was toward the end of second grade when my legs began to bother me. We lived in a small house on Grace Mill Village, located near the big city of Rutherfordton, NC. My school was less than a mile from my home, so I walked to school with the other kids from the village. School would be out for the summer in a couple of weeks, and boy was I looking forward to that. But the persistent pain in my knees was getting worse with each passing day.

On one occasion, when I was having lunch at my grandmother's home, which was located next door to my school, I complained to Grandma Ford that my knees were bothering me.

"Oh, don't worry about that Bob, it's just growing pains," she replied.

"Well, if that's what it is, then this growing up stuff is going to kill me," I replied.

We had a short discussion as to why growing up had to be so painful, and the final deduction was that this is just how life is, end of discussion.

I continued my daily trips to school and back, complaining to whoever would listen to me, which was not that many people. My mother, following the advice of my grandma that it was all about growing pains, did not seem to be too alarmed by my aches and pains. But as my condition got even more painful, and my complaining got more persistent, my mother decided that it was time to take me to a doctor.

I really did not like the sound of going to see a doctor, but since I had a lot of growing up to do, I did not want to be in all this pain throughout the process. Dr. Logan, at least in my eyes, was a big man with a stern-looking face. I was afraid of him, but since my mother was there with me, I tolerated the visit to his office. I can't remember all the tests he performed on me that day, but his diagnosis was that I had a bad case of rheumatic fever.

I had never heard of this disease before. All I knew was that I didn't feel like I had a fever. My mother was instructed to take me home and put me in bed for the next three months. Bed rest was the remedy. All I had to do was lie around in bed for three months during the summer when school was out, and all the kids in the village were out riding their bikes and going swimming and playing "cowboys and Indians" and "hide-and-go-seek" in the late afternoon, and baseball down in the old cow pasture. Yep, all I had to do that summer was just lie back and watch the rest of the mill village kids have all the fun in the world. What could be simpler than this? It would be like falling off a log. Why, I bet it wouldn't take more than a year or so for those three months to pass by.

Trying to get an eight-year-old to be still for a few minutes was difficult enough for my parents, so this was going to be a big challenge for them, as well as for me. My teachers had already complained that I wouldn't stay in my seat. So, I was a little on the hyperactive side of life. Keeping me in bed for three months was going to be an enormous challenge. I thought that this was a good time to ask my parents for a new TV set, and to my surprise, they agreed. They had been talking about getting a TV set for some time, so now was a good time to do that. It worked! Neither my parents nor I went crazy that summer.

I did have one "lo-co moment" though. My mother went down to Johnson's Grocery Store located just down the street from us. While she was away, I got to thinking how long it had been since I had gotten dirty. At that moment I had a strong urge to go outside and roll around in the dirt, just to see how it felt. It felt great! Boy, how I had missed being dirty. Upon her return from the store, my mother was a little upset with me, but not too much so.

I think she knew how important it was for an eight-year-old boy to get dirty every now and then. She probably told me not to do it again, which I didn't. At the end of the summer, Dr. Logan let me go back to school. There was one stipulation: I was not allowed to run and play at recess. I had to watch the action from the sidelines. Unfortunately, my rheumatic fever had left me with a heart murmur. I would be under this duress for quite some time.

Mom got the word out to all the women on the village to call me down if they saw me running. I had strange women I had never met before come to their front door and call out to me, "Bob, stop running!" Dang, I couldn't get away with anything. Mom had too many good connections.

Well, I remember my grandma's words that it was growing pains, and sure enough it was. At some point in my middle teens, I outgrew the murmur to the point that my doctor could no longer hear that funny little noise. I went on to have rheumatic fever two other times, with the same prescription—stay in bed—and each time I would spend an entire summer watching the world go by.

I learned early on that growing up has its challenges and, after growing up, I discovered that life in general has its challenges. Grandma gave some good advice on how to deal with life. I think it matches up with the teachings of Jesus when he said that (my paraphrasing of Luke 9:62): "No one can live a productive, meaningful life by looking back at what could have been, because this person is no good for themselves, or anyone else for that matter, and certainly not for the Lord's work."

Jesus was saying that we cannot live in the past. We need to be in the present moment of life. We can't keep looking back wishing and hoping that things were different. As my Grandma Ford was saying, "Life is what is." When we accept life in this way, then we are empowered to be transformed by the events of life, rather than be overcome by them.

23

Hide and Go Seek

A cotton mill village in Western North Carolina was a perfect place for an only child to grow up. The village was full of kids of all ages. In the warm summer months, a popular game in the village was "hide-and-go-seek." One person, who was the designated "It," would hide his/her face and count down from 100, while the rest of us hid. In some of the games, "It" would find everyone, but on some occasions there would be someone who could not be found. I can remember a game or two in which everyone quit playing the game and went home while I was still hiding out there somewhere. Eventually, I realized that the other kids had forgotten about me and had gone home. So, I would come out of my hiding place and go home, too. Besides, it was getting dark anyway. Such was the game of the mill village kids.

The Gospel accounts of Resurrection Sunday inform us that a number of folks were out looking for Jesus. Strangely enough, Jesus found them. Some were even looking in the wrong place and Jesus still found them. Thus was the case of Mary of Magdalene. Early Resurrection morning, she went looking for Jesus in the graveyard, but could not find him. It was there that she met a stranger, who called her by name. She met someone who knew all about her—the good, the bad, and the ugly. She could not recognize him at first, but then she was given "spiritual sight," which allowed her to see this activity of God that had drawn near to her. At that point, she was liberated from her fears and ran to tell others of her life-changing experience.

In another place nearby, some of the disciples who had locked themselves in the upper room were hiding from the people who had put the Lord to death. They were afraid of what was going to happen to them. Would they, too, be crucified? Jesus came to them in their self-imposed tomb and liberated them, telling them to go forth into the world and to proclaim the Good News.

The story of Adam and Eve is one of hiding from God. They were afraid to face God because of what they had done with their lives. They did not like themselves, and they were sure that God did not like them either. Hidden away in the bushes, they heard the footsteps of the Lord coming through the garden calling out to them, "Where are you?"

The fact of the matter is that we, too, can hide from ourselves, from others, and from God. God will not force us to come out of our hiding places. The Good News of Easter is that God is looking for us, inviting us to come out of our hiding places, and to meet him and discover what He can do with our lives. This is the Good News of Easter, that we have been liberated and there is no need to hide anymore.

24

Hope for the Hopeless

There was once a man who lived in a faraway land. One day he heard a knock at his door. When he opened the door, he found it was the Lord who had come for a visit. "Come in," the man said, but the Lord declined the offer.

"I have something I want to show you," replied the Lord. "Grab your hat and coat and come with me."

So the man did as he was told, and he and the Lord walked down a pathway together. Soon they came to a big valley, and they walked around for a while in silence. Then the Lord said, "Mortal Man, what do you see in this valley?"

The man replied, "Nothing but bones, Lord, just a bunch of dry bones that seem to cover the ground everywhere."

"You're right, Mortal Man, that's all they are, just a bunch of dry bones," replied the Lord.

The Lord then made a request, "I have something I want you to do for me."

The man replied, "Yes, Lord, anything you ask I will try to do."

"This is what I want you to do," replied the Lord. "I want you to preach to these bones."

While the man agreed to do this, he wondered in his heart what good it would do.

The Lord said, "Tell these dry bones that they are going to live again. I am going to give them new life. Tell them that for Me."

The man stepped forward a few steps, cleared his throat a few times and took a deep breath, then said:

"OK, dry bones, I don't know if you can hear me or not, and if you can I'm not sure that you would believe me, but I have some Good News for you today. All of you dry bones are going to be born again. You are going to experience new life, but I really don't know how this is going to happen. This is what the Lord wanted me to tell you today—that, believe it or not, you are going to live again."

The man had barely gotten the words out of his mouth, when a faint noise started coming up from the ground, and became louder and louder, until it was almost deafening. It was the sound of all the bones moving around and coming together. Soon all the bones were all covered with muscle and skin. They looked okay from the outside, but there was something still not quite right. They seemed to be missing something.

The man replied, "Lord, I don't believe that there is any life in them."

"You're right," replied the Lord, "that's why I have something else I want you to do for Me."

The man agreed to do whatever the Lord wanted him to do.

"Here is what I want you to do," replied the Lord. "I want you to talk to the Wind for Me. Tell the Wind to come from all directions upon the face of the Earth. Tell the Wind to blow upon these dry bones."

Again, the man stepped forward a few steps, cleared his throat and said, "OK Wind, wherever You are, come and blow upon these dry bones. This is what the Lord wanted me to say to You, so if You can hear me, just do what the Lord is asking You to do."

As soon as the man had gotten these words out of his mouth, the Wind began to pick up, and soon there was a great rushing of the Wind in all directions upon the face of the Earth, blowing across the dry bones.

Then suddenly, the dry bones took on new life. They stood upright and began to walk around the valley. That which had been dead had come back to life. That which had been lost had been found. Those who had lost their humanity found it again that day. Those who had had no hope now were filled with hope and possibilities. The weak had become strong. The defeated ones had overcome the chaos that had come upon them.

This picture of the activity of God among His people is found in the Book of Ezekiel. It is a picture of God who won't let go, won't give up on His people, no matter what their life situation might be. It is a picture of God the Spirit, the Wind, breathing new life into His people who had lost all hope of having a life.

This is not a picture of a once-in-a-lifetime event. Instead, it represents the ongoing activity of God in all generations. In the midst of our most chaotic times, God is present. He is at work bringing forth new life out of tragic situations. We are reminded here that this is the same God of Creation, Who overcame the initial chaos and brought forth life. This is the God who brings hope for the hopeless.

25

How Much Does It Cost?

He was an ordained minister, although this was not the vocation his parents would have chosen for him. His father was a medical doctor, and his mother, a teacher. He had uncles and aunts on both sides of the family who were in prominent professional positions, so it was expected that he, too, would follow suit.

One of the unique things about this man was his ability to do what he wanted to do, rather than do what others felt he ought to be doing. Some would say that he marched to the beat of a different drummer. He was, indeed, his own man.

During his early thirties, his country went to war. It was not a war provoked by another nation or nations, but one that came from the desires of the political leaders of his country. The odd thing about this war was that not only were enemy soldiers put into prison camps, but a large number of the citizens of his country were put into prison camps as well. Generally, the military needs all the manpower it can get, but not so in this war.

This minister, born into a privileged family with all the potential and possibilities that were afforded to him, decided to put his life on the line. He decided to join a group of citizens who were committed to bringing an end to the political leaders who had taken the country down a very destructive pathway. Their plans were to kill these political leaders in the hope of ending the death and destruction that had been brought upon their people and others around them.

There would be a great risk in attempting to bring this about, but they deemed that it was worth whatever cost they might have to pay. The plan was set and put in place, but as fate would have it, it did not work. Unfortunately for them, they were linked to these efforts, and were soon arrested and put in jail. Some were put to death early on, while others spent time in various prison camps and other facilities.

The minister, after spending a considerable amount of time in prison, was put to death near the end of the war. His captors stripped him of his clothes and marched him to the gallows to be hanged. It is said that when the guards arrived at his cell, that they found him on his knees, praying for those who would put him to death. Dietrich Bonhoeffer was thirty-nine years old.

Recorded in the Gospel accounts of the life and times of Jesus are a number of sayings that reflect the need to count the cost of following Him. On one particular day, a multitude of people were gathered around Jesus, seeking, I suppose, something from Him that would make their lives better. As recorded in Luke 14:28-33 (my paraphrasing), in the midst of this gathering, Jesus turned and said to them:

Which of you, intending to build a house does not take the time to sit down and figure out just how much it's going to cost to build it? You don't want to start the building process and then find out you don't have enough money to finish it. . . . So likewise, those of you who think you want to follow me, need to stop and consider what it might cost, lest you start the journey with me and then find out that you are not willing to pay the cost to finish out the journey.

How much does it cost? Jesus asks for all of our mind, body, and spirit. Nothing less will do.

Our Lord demands all that we have, and then gives to us what He demands. The bottom line is, when we go to check out of this life, we will find that our bill has already been paid.

26

Hub-Bah Hub-Bah Ice Cream

School would be out in a couple of weeks, and I had no plans at all for the summer. A friend of mine, Louie Ballard, had applied for a job with a local ice cream company and was scheduled to start work as soon as school was out. He said that they were looking for another driver to make rounds through the various communities of Spartanburg, South Carolina.

Selling ice cream sounded like a winner for me, so I went to put my application in at Hub-Bah Hub-Bah Ice Cream Company. Desperate to find a driver, they hired me. Each driver was assigned to a particular area in and around the city. We were known as the Hub-Bah Hub-Bah Ice Cream Men. A music box in the cab played a tune that would let children and parents know that we were near.

At the beginning of each street, I paused for about a minute or two to give the children time to convince their parents they needed ice cream. Slowly, I drove down each street, giving both children and adults time to come out to the road. Man, selling ice cream on a hot summer day was as easy as falling off a log.

I went into all neighborhoods in my allotted area. In some areas, a group of kids would come up to my truck wanting to see all the different flavors. They made their purchase and off they went. On several occasions, the smallest and generally the youngest kid in the group would come up last and hold up a small hand that contained about 2 or 3 cents. Most of the ice cream cost 50 cents or more, but I would take their 2 or 3 cents and allow them to pick out whatever they wanted. In fact, this scenario was played out on a rather regular basis. I was determined that any kid who came to my ice cream truck would not be disappointed. Whatever amount of money they had I would accept as payment.

Needless to say, I didn't make a lot of money that summer. In fact, there were weeks that I owed the ice cream company more money than I made in the week. No, I didn't make a lot of money, but I had a lot of fun and enjoyment selling ice cream to the kids, and even at times giving it away at my own expense.

I am reminded of the scripture from the Prophet Isaiah where he writes in Isaiah 55:1 (my paraphrasing):

"Hey! Everyone who thirsts for life! Come to the Living Waters. Come, you that have no money. Come eat and enjoy. Yes, come and take all the good stuff you want. Without money and without price!"

We are invited to Abundant Life. If it had a price, we couldn't afford it, but not to worry, it's free. While many times free stuff means cheap stuff that no one else wants, that is not so with the life that God offers to us. Like the wine served at the wedding feast that Jesus attended, it was the best in the entire world.

To have abundant life is to allow ourselves to be embraced by God the Father. It is to receive His love, grace, mercy and forgiveness into our life. It means, as Paul Tillich would say, that we accept our acceptance. We are forgiven. We are loved.

This is no "cheap grace." It is "costly grace," but the price has been paid. When we get to the checkout counter, we discover that someone else has picked up the bill for us. Yes, the true Hub-Bah, Hub-Bah Man has come to town, and we are invited to eat and enjoy life to the fullest. Yes, feast on the One who has given to us freely.

27

Hunting Squirrels

Three of my friends and I decided to go squirrel hunting one Saturday morning in the early fall. Since one friend had a relative who owned a small cabin in the woods not far from Spartanburg, SC, we decided to spend the night there and get up early the next morning to start our day of intense hunting.

That particular Saturday morning found us roaming through the woods with our .22 rifles in hand, looking for any signs of squirrels. The theory we were operating on was that squirrels were up early in the day and that was the best time to spot one, but the theory just wasn't working for us that day.

Eventually, about mid-morning, a voice rang out, "Squirrel!" We all came running down a small incline to a big oak tree. At the very top of the tree was a squirrel. We positioned ourselves around the tree, one of us on each side. At the count of three, we began to fire our weapons. During this assault, the squirrel made his way down the tree, until he arrived at the bottom. Not a bullet had touched him. He calmly scampered away through the underbrush without a mark on his body.

Okay, we were not David Crockett or Daniel Boone, but we gave it our best effort. Looking back on our hunting experience, we were amazed that the squirrel did not find four dead bodies when he got to the bottom of the oak tree. As we followed the squirrel down the tree, and fired as he went from top to bottom of the tree, the only thing preventing us from shooting one another was the tree.

The fact that we didn't shoot one another is still puzzling to me. We just weren't thinking about what we were doing and the danger we were putting ourselves in at the time. Accidents of this nature happen every year somewhere in the country. Why not us?

There have been books written about bad things happening to good people. Yet, these things happen quite often. Some call them accidents, while others call them God's will. I don't know the answer to the question, "Why do bad things happen to good people?"

While I don't have an answer to that question, I believe that there is an answer to the question, "In light of surviving this experience, what is it that God wants me to do with the rest of my life?" If we are willing to wrestle with that question, then I think that we may find an answer.

Victor Frankl in his book, *Man's Search for Meaning*, says that the question to ask is: "What do I still have to give back to my family, community, or country in spite of all that has been taken from me?"

The Apostle Paul says in his letter to the Romans that there is nothing that can separate us from the love of God in Christ Jesus. The call of God to the Christian Way or Journey is one full of uncertainties. While we can't predict the future, we can know the One Who holds us in His future.

28

I Can't Do That!

It was my first year in school at Ruth Elementary School. As if that were not enough pressure on a seven-year-old, my mom volunteered me for a part in a "Tom Thumb Wedding." I was to be the "ring-bearer," so all I had to do was walk down the aisle in the school auditorium to make my way up on stage, and stand there until the rings were needed. Simple as falling off a log! Only one thing stood in the way of this scenario: I didn't want to do it. I protested to anyone who would listen to me, but all I got was encouragement to do what I had been asked to do. Rats, it seems sometimes that the entire world is against you.

This event was a big community enterprise, so a number of rehearsals were scheduled to ensure that nothing went wrong. On a day that a rehearsal was planned, I went down to my grandparents' home, which was located next to our school. After having the lunch my Grandma Ford had prepared for me, I informed her that I wasn't going back to school. I told her that I did not want to be in that wedding, and I was not going to the rehearsal that afternoon.

At about that time there was a knock on the door, and two girls from the school had come to get me. I was doomed; there was no way out of this situation. The girls were not going back to school without me, and after all, they were bigger than I, so I went quietly.

Back at the school, everyone had gathered in the auditorium waiting on guess who to show up. Taking my place at the entrance of the auditorium, I slowly proceeded down the aisle and took my place on the stage with the other members of the wedding party.

I have pictures of that event that were taken by the local newspaper out of Rutherfordton, NC. There I was dressed in my white shorts and shirt, holding the rings on a pillow and looking okay. The program went off as planned.

There have been other opportunities set before me that I did not want to do, but someone believed in me and encouraged me to give it a try and I did. Sometimes God speaks to us through other people. Sometimes other people can see something in us that we cannot see for ourselves. As the saying goes, we live too close to the woods to see the trees.

I believe that these folks who show up in our life do so not by accident, but by God's design. When faced with a great challenge in life, we choose to run away from it, but it seems that God has a way of intervening in our lives. I believe that He is always seeking to take us from where we are today to where we need to be tomorrow. To accomplish this, He uses people around us to help us face up to the challenges of life.

At a later point in time, when we look back over our life's

journey, perhaps we pause to give thanks to those who God has allowed to cross our pathway at the right time. You can say that this is simply luck, or you may decide that it was the hand of God that was guiding and directing your life through some challenge set before you.

I have discovered, as others have discovered, that what God asks of us, He provides us. Therefore, whatever challenges may come, He will provide a way for us to deal with and overcome them. On numerous occasions, God speaks through various ways that He will never forsake us or leave us, no matter what is going on in our lives. "I can't do that" becomes, with God's help, "I can do all things that He wills for my life."

29

Is This Equipment Necessary?

He was just a kid, a teenager at best, and now he found himself facing the battle of his life. He was just doing his duty of helping his father and brothers out during a serious conflict with some intruders. They had been involved in this conflict for days, and their supply of food was running out, so the youngest member of the family came to the rescue. Among his family at the front lines of battle, he had felt a strong urge to get involved.

It seems that they were faced with overwhelming odds. The enemy, big and strong beyond measure, had offered up their best. "Come out and face me," was the challenge that could be heard from the battlefield. This guy was like a Sherman tank with armor from head to toe. There were no apparent weaknesses. How could anyone survive an encounter with this giant of a man? So, there was a standoff. Each side was just standing there, staring at one another from across the battlefield.

The young boy looked around, and saw that no one from his side of the battlefield was making a move. Who would take the challenge? Fear had such a hold on them that no one was willing to step up and take this challenger on. No one, that is, except this kid, this youngster who was left at home because he was so young and small of frame. "I'll go," he said!

"You've got to be kidding!" said his brothers.

"No, I'm not! I can do this."

Unable to deter the youngster from his decision to go into battle with a man ten times his size, his father took armor from another soldier and placed it on his son. "Ok, now, go out to battle. May God be with you," was the blessing given by his father.

With his armor from head to toe, the young man made his move or at least tried to make his move, but he could not. The weight of the armor was such that he could not walk with it on him. He would have to go to plan B. Just give me my sling and a few rocks he says to his father. So out steps a young man with just a sling and a few rocks. He walks slowly toward the enemy, studying his opponent with each step.

Laughter can be heard from the other side of the field. A voice can be heard, "You send a child to do a man's work? Is this the best you have to send?"

Still the youngster comes closer and closer at a steady pace. His eyes are focused, and there is a look of determination on his face. He will not allow himself to be influenced by the laughter and mockery. At this point, survival is not an issue. He is willing to die for this cause. He is determined that there will be two dead bodies on the field when it is all over.

At fifty yards, he makes his move. With his sling in hand, he places a stone in it and takes aim. Steady, steady he twirls the sling and releases the stone. There is a whistling sound as the stone makes its way across the field. Appearing to be suspended in time, the rock finds its mark. An "Achilles Heel" located between the eyes is the mark that was found. It was the only place that would accommodate the stone's arrival.

Like a giant oak tree and the walls of Jericho, the giant who was bigger than life came tumbling down. Great was his fall, and the sound of it thundered across the battlefield. It could be heard for miles and miles. So there on the battlefield, where men go to do war, a young man stood. The trophy was his. That which had opposed his people was now lying dead before him. Those who came with this giant of a man had fled back into the woods. The sense of victory embraced him as adrenaline rushed through his veins.

He thought he would die, but he lived. The morning breeze invigorated his soul. Tears came into his eyes, and he felt the exhaustion of mind, body, and spirit. Before this encounter, he felt a power and strength in his body, but now he felt vulnerable and weak.

When he rejoined his father and brothers, he was received as an equal. He had earned his place among the men of the family. He left home a boy; he returned a man. Although still in his teens, the childhood things would be left behind. He could not go back to what once was home. He would leave father and mother and establish his own place.

When these moments come in life, you know that it is time to move on. It is all about the process of our journey in life and the challenges we face. It is the cutting of the umbilical cord and being set free.

The question is, what equipment do we need to take with us? Many a young man and many a young woman have gone out from home to set the world on fire, but unfortunately for them, they had to come back home for more matches. In the spiritual sense, the Apostle Paul provides us with a list of items we will need in order to meet the challenges that we will encounter in life.

You may find this scripture in Ephesians 6:10-20:

"Be strong in the Lord and in the power of His might. Put on the whole armor of God, that you may be able to stand up against the seductive powers of evil. . . .Gird your waist with truth.

"Put on the breastplate of right living. Covering your feet with the Gospel of Peace; Taking the shield of faith and the helmet of salvation and the sword of the Spirit."

Is all this equipment necessary? You be the judge!

30

Just a Piece of Glass

Mrs. Englewood had gathered items throughout her house to use in the upcoming yard sale. The house was just too full of junk, and it was time to get rid of some of this stuff. She collected items large and small. They were items that were no longer used by the family members, so no need to keep them around. Come Saturday, all the items were neatly placed on tables on the front lawn and driveway. Signs placed throughout the community read "Big Yard Sale, Five Decades of Collective Junk."

The day of the yard sale was not disappointing. Hundreds of folks from all around the Shelby, Nc, community made their way to the Englewood Yard Sale. One particular lady from another community, by the name of Mrs. Jones stopped by and took a good look over the various offerings of the day. On one of the tables, she spotted a round paperweight, which had a price tag of fifty cents. It contained an array of colors and seemed nice enough to fit on the coffee table back home. She bought the item and took it home.

Several years later, a friend from New York City came for a visit. During her stay, the friend noticed the round paperweight and asked Mrs. Jones where she had purchased it? She told her friend from New York about the numerous yard sales throughout her community during the summer months.

The friend's husband dealt in antiques, and she asked if she could take the paperweight back with her to New York to let him have a look at it. Her request was granted, and after several weeks went by with no word, Mrs. Jones assumed that the verdict on the paperweight was that it was just a piece of glass.

Then one day she received a phone call from her friend in New York. The appraisal was that the paperweight was worth somewhere "between twelve and fifteen." Well, this was good news for Mrs. Jones ,who commented that she had only paid fifty cents for it, so a twelve-to- fifteen-dollar profit was not too bad.

"No! No!" replied her friend. "I mean twelve to fifteen thousand dollars. This paperweight was made sometime back in the 16th century, and it is a very rare piece of glass, and there should be no problem finding a buyer if you want to sell it."

Sometimes things are not what they appear to be. A piece of glass to the untrained eye; but from the eye of an experienced antique dealer, the value was obvious.

It is one thing to misjudge a piece of glass as to its true value and worth, but quite another thing when we misjudge the value and worth of another human being. In the New Testament, there are stories of a number of people who were thought to be just about worthless by many people in their community.

John 4 tells the story of the woman at the well, who went there each day by herself because none of the other ladies in the village would have anything to do with her. Luke 19 tells the story of a Jewish tax collector, who was hated by all of his fellow countrymen because he had over-taxed them.

Both of these individuals were considered to be worthless human beings, if, that is, they were even afforded that status. Yet, Jesus saw something of value and worth in both of them. The woman at the well is thought to be Mary Magdalene, who became the first person to proclaim the Good News (Gospel) after the Resurrectionof Christ. Jesus went to the home of Zacchaeus, the tax collector, to have Communion (a meal) with him and his family.

These acts of Jesus toward the outcasts and untouchables of the community indicate that what the world sees as worthless and undesirable, Jesus saw as having value and worth. They were the kind of people you expect to find discarded at a yard sale.

Unfortunately, we have not moved too far down the road. Today there are a number of people who have been written off as worthless and no good for anything. The most prominent of these are the "homeless folks" who have no place to call home and no place to go when they are forced to leave the shelter where they stay at night. A number of these folks are homeless veterans who have served our country and now have to deal with the scars of war. They are the folks that cities and communities wish would just go away. They are often seen as parasites by local, state, and national government political leaders.

If we take the Book of Genesis with any seriousness, the fact that God made all human beings in His image implies a value and worth that are inherent in all people. To dehumanize anyone is a denial of God's creative work. It has been said that we are all connected, whether we are black or white or brown, it doesn't matter. We are connected, because God the Father is the connecting link.

Just a piece of glass, I don't think so. There was value and worth unseen and undetected. Look around you, attempt to see the world as God sees it. See it with the eyes of compassion, love, grace, and mercy and see what a difference it will make in you.

31

Luck or Divine Intervention

It was the last class for me on Friday morning, before a quick trip through the CID Student Center at Gardner-Webb College to grab a sandwich and then off to work. As I was leaving the Student Center, one of my classmates stopped me to ask what I would be doing over the weekend.

"I am off to work now, but what did you have in mind?"

Well, it seems that Jackie Millwood had gotten himself in a bind. He was scheduled to sing with a Gospel Quartet that he belonged to and he had also made a commitment to go on a FOCUS Trip (Fellowship of Christians United in Service) to Hickory, Nc, that weekend. I agreed that it would be difficult for him to be at both places over the weekend, and apologized that I could not sing, so taking his place on the quartet was out of the question.

So with that settled, he asked me to take his place on the

FOCUS Team to Hickory. I explained to him that I was off to work on top of Hog Back Mountain and would not be coming back down until late Saturday afternoon around 4 or 5 o'clock p.m. He informed me that he was scheduled to speak at Longview Baptist Church on Sunday morning, as part of a Youth Emphasis Weekend. Services would be held on Friday and Saturday night, with the final service taking place on Sunday morning.

Yes, I could be there by Sunday morning, but I had never been to Hickory before in my life. So, I did not have a clue on how to get there. He made me a quick map and off we went to our respective obligations.

My trip to Hickory on late Saturday afternoon started out okay, but not being sure if I were going in the right direction, I stopped at a gas station and asked for an update on how I was doing. It seems that I had gotten off track just a bit and needed to make some navigational adjustments.

I continued my journey toward Hickory and the Longview Community and arrived after dark.

Now, all I had to do was find Longview Baptist Church. A sign on Highway 70 pointed to a street that would lead in the direction of the church. Continuing up that road, I finally came to a stop sign, but still had not seen a church. So, I went back down the road in the hope of finding the church that I had apparently missed. At the end of the road, still no luck.

Eventually I spotted a building with a lot of cars parked around it. Although there was no steeple, it was the only building on the street that held some possibilities of being the church I was looking for. I drove back and forth through the parking lot to make sure that it was indeed a church. Finally, I was able to get a view of the person in the pulpit, and recognized my fellow student, Larry Thomas. I was at the right place.

I made my way into the church, via the back entrance. The service was just about over, since it had taken me quite some time to find this place. The final prayer being said, I walked into the sanctuary to introduce myself to the FOCUS Team. Standing near the FOCUS team members was a young lady from the church who caught my eye.

Later on in the evening, I was informed that I would be staying with the Newton family, along with a music major, Steve Little. When I arrived, I discovered that this was the home of the young lady I had briefly met at church. It was not the norm for male members of a FOCUS Team to be housed in the home of a female youth, but I didn't put up a fuss about it, and neither did Steve.

After the service on Sunday morning and lunch at Mull's Restaurant, it was time to head back to Boiling Springs. Before I left, Wayne and Juanita Newton invited me to come back. I don't know if they were just being cordial, or if they really meant it, but anyway, I immediately took them up on their offer. Eventually the young lady, whose name is Gail, and I started dating. Three years later, we were married at Long View Baptist Church, and now have been married for 37 years.

Was this just luck or was it Divine Intervention? Does this sort of thing just happen once in awhile, or is it an ongoing activity of God? In the poem, "The Hound of Heaven," Francis Thompson presents the thought that God is ever in pursuit of us, always seeking to bring us from where we are to where we need to be.

Jesus compared us to a herd of sheep, which are some of the most vulnerable animals on the face of the earth. They are prone to getting lost, and if attacked, they simply sit down. If we are more like sheep than any other animal, then indeed, our Good Shepherd must be at all times intervening in our life, knowing that we need all the help we can get.

In our journey through life, we experience at times its good, bad, and ugly sides. In the midst of these events, it is difficult sometimes to determine what God is doing with us. The promise that He has made to all of us is that He will never leave or forsake us.

While at times we may feel lost and all alone, we are never alone. God is always present with us, seeking to bless us and guide us into a meaningful life. This is not just luck; it is Divine Intervention.

32

No Longer Needed

It was a typical Wednesday for me at the hospital where I had served as Director of Pastoral Care for nearly twenty-four years. I made my usual rounds to the various critical care units and took a walk through the emergency department to assess patient and family needs. Along the way, I stopped by the Admitting Department to pick up the admit forms that had come in overnight.

I had come in that day later than my usual 8:00 a.m. due to a minor accident my wife had been involved in the day before. I had taken our car to have the damages appraised and then to the body shop. Since I then had to travel to a car rental facility, it was nearly 11:30 a.m. by the time I arrived at my office. After going into my email system, I discovered I had an appointment with my supervisor. That was unusual, because our scheduled monthly meeting was the second Monday of each month and this was Wednesday, August 31. I looked at my watch and realized that I still had a few minutes to make the meeting on time.

Upon my arrival at HR, I was instructed to go to the conference room where my supervisor would meet me momentarily. On the way over, I had pondered in my mind what this might be about. Maybe one of my forty-five member staff had done something wrong, or one of the local ministers was upset about a patient not being available for him/her to visit. Beyond these two suspicions, I did not have a clue.

Soon my supervisor arrived with a handful of papers. I was asked if I had read my emails that day, and I said "No." My next response was, "If I had read them, which one is it that you are referring to?"

"The one that our CEO sent out this morning," was my supervisor's reply.

"No, I did not read that one, but if I had, what would it have told me?" was my response.

What I heard then fell on me like a ton of bricks. The hospital was downsizing by thirty-six staff, and I was one of them.

"You've got to be kidding," I said. I felt like my world had dropped out from under me. How could this be, I wondered. Just a few weeks before, I had spent about an hour or more with the Chief Operating Officer (COO) looking for new space to put the new chapel. Prior to that, the COO and my supervisor had come to view a presentation that one of my staff had put together for me on how a new chapel would look and the potential for ministry that it would provide for the hospital staff, the patients and their family members. Now I was being told that my job was ending at 6:00 p.m. that evening, but I could take the rest of the day off if I wanted to do so.

After shedding a few tears, I got my composure back and asked what I needed to do next. There was a document of about eight to ten pages that I needed to read and sign before the following Friday. Also, I could take my time cleaning out my office, there was no hurry. I did take the rest of the day off and met with my wife for lunch and discussed our financial situation.

There is no easy way of dealing with being let go from your place of employment. Depression was more at work in me than anything else. A lot of my identity had been connected to my work as chaplain at this hospital; now that was gone. Some people leave one job and the next day they have another. I knew that it would not be like that for me, and it wasn't.

I am a strong believer that God is never finished with us, although others might be. I did not know what He might have in mind for me, but I believed that something would come along, and it did. It was not what I had expected, but I believe that it was where God wanted me to be. The Reverend Susan Smith, a female minister friend of mine, approached me about helping her with "homeless veterans" in our community. The opportunity sounded interesting, so I said yes to the offer.

The place was called "Grace House," and it was where homeless people met each day, Monday through Friday, for shelter from 7:00 a.m. to 5:00 p.m. Grace House provided food, drinks, restrooms, a lounge with a TV and computer and a lot of support from the staff. We started meeting with the homeless veterans each week on

Wednesday from 12:00 noon to 1:00 p.m. It was a time for those who would risk coming to our meeting to share issues, concerns and needs.

The group grew from two or three to about fifteen to twenty in a short time. Word was getting out that we were helping folks find jobs and places to stay instead of the woods. Others who had a heart for veterans joined us, and eventually representatives from various agencies that provide assistance to veterans started to attend our meetings. Out of this group came the personnel and resources to provide a "Stand Down" for veterans in need at the local fair grounds. A "Stand Down" event provides various services, i.e., medical and dental care, clothing, and food to homeless veterans.

Scripture tells us that God works in mysterious ways His will to perform. From a place where I heard the words "you're not needed anymore" to a place where I am told that "this is where God wants you to be, we need you here" has been a journey through the "valley of fear, uncertainty, and doubt" to the "mountaintop of dreams, hopes, and healing."

When one door closes, if we look around, we will find that another door has opened. Our life journey presents us with various challenges. We do not always get what we want, but God always gives us what we need. In our journey, we will discover that God is always in the business of Up-Sizing workers for His vineyard (a biblical term). Many times what God has for us to do is not what we had in mind. While rejection may appear to us as a "dead-end street," God makes it the source of our greatest blessing.

There are some basic needs of all human beings: one is to be needed, another is to be accepted, and yet another is to feel that our life has value. The Good News is about all of the above.

33

Not Smart Enough

My grandparents, Manley and Bessie Ford, lived next door to Ruth Elementary School, so it was that all the Ford kids went to this school. I'm not saying that the Ford kids were not smart, but of seven children, only one finished high school. Of course, those were different days and different times when not much emphasis was placed on education. The focus was more on what needed to be done on the farm. The main priority was making a living, with education coming in at second or third place.

My father, Ralph William Ford, had a most difficult time in school, and the 3rd grade seemed to be the worst. It took him three years to complete that grade. One teacher, Miss McFarland, taught all the Ford kids. Those must have been very trying times for her. Year after year she would say, "Well, I suppose this is the last of the Fords," then one more would show up. There was a span of eight years, when no Fords came through the system. Then I came along.

I don't really know what my uncles and aunts did to Miss

McFarland, but I believe that she saw me as the last hope of getting back at the Ford Family for all the difficulty they had inflicted upon her life. So, this is the way it went that year. She had the room set up with the smartest kids on the row next to the windows. The other rows were in descending order according to how smart she thought the student to be.

I ended up on the row next to the door. During the afternoon session, she would allow kids on the same row and adjacent rows to study together on the next day's homework. The problem that I faced was I was the only kid on my row, and the next row was empty. I went up to Miss McFarland's desk and asked if I could move over to the row next to James and Leroy. Her response was plain and simple, "No, there is no need of you causing them to fail like you are doing. You're not as smart as they are, so go back to your desk and do the best you can."

Well, that took a big load off my back. I thought I had to compete with all the other kids in order to pass to the 4th grade. It was not a surprise to me that I did not pass the 3rd grade. Had it not been for the post-WWII generation, I would have been required to do the 3rd grade over again, but since there was no room for me in the Inn (3rd grade), I was moved up to the 4th grade on a trial basis.

In the 4th grade, Mrs. Logan was my teacher. I don't how many of the Fords she had to deal with over the years, but it seemed she had no resilient animosity for the Ford Family and me in particular. I passed 4th grade and went on to become the president of my class in the 5th grade. Life was getting better.

I have long ago passed through Miss McFarland's class, but her voice from the past still haunts me today, "Bob, you're not smart enough." What I have learned to do through the years, with some help from my friends, is to challenge those voices from my past. These negative thoughts, if left unchallenged, will take control and prevent us from realizing our full potential.

In his book, *The Power of Now*, Eckhart Tolle says that we are more than our thoughts. He suggests that we need to listen to our thoughts as an "Outsider" and know that our thoughts are not all of whom and what we are in this world. This practice gives us some space between our true self and our thoughts. This spacing is called "the gap," which, with practice, becomes wider and wider.

I am reminded of the scripture from Proverbs 23:7, which says "for whatever thoughts we have in our heart, so we become." In the computer world, the saying goes, "junk in, junk out." The scripture in Psalm 119:105 says of the Lord, "Thy Word is a Lamp unto my feet, and a Light unto my path." If we listen to that Word, it will tell us that we ought not to underestimate what God can do with our lives. In spite of the negative voices from the past that keep telling us we can't, God's voice in the present moment says clearly that we can do that which He calls us to do.

"Hear oh hear, all of you that have ears to hear what the Lord is saying!"

34

Once I Was Blind, but Now I See

Once upon a time in a faraway village, there lived a man who was blind. He had been this way from birth and had to beg for a living. One day, a stranger came through town and saw his condition. Those traveling with the stranger thought that the man must have done something wrong to be in that condition, but they were informed that was not the case. The stranger spat upon the ground and rubbed the moistened soil together and put the mud on the blind man's eyes.

Following instructions, the blind man went to a specific pool of water to wash his eyes, and discovered that he could see.

You would think that everyone in the village would be very happy for the man who was once blind, but now could see, but they were not. In fact, they were very upset with him. Some said that this was not the same man; he was someone who just looked like the other man. When the man told them how it was that he was able to see, the people became even more suspicious of him. They eventually took him to the religious authorities in the village and explained the situation to them. They, too, wanted to know what had happened. The man said that he did not have all the answers to their questions, but one thing he did know was that "once I was blind, but now I see."

The authorities went to the man's parents and asked them, "What is going on with your son?" The parents did not know. The only thing they knew was that he was born blind. How he came to see, they had no idea.

Again the religious leaders went back to the man and asked the same questions. They were also upset that this whole thing had happened on the Holy Day of the week. This time the man's response was that the stranger who had healed him must be a prophet. The authorities could take no more of this and banned him from the religious center.

When the stranger heard about this, he returned to the village and came to the man he had helped. The stranger asked the man, "Do you believe in me?" To this the man replied, "Yes Lord, I believe" He then fell down and worshipped him.

There is movement in two directions in this story. The man born blind moves in the direction of The Light and sees, while the other folks move in the direction of darkness and go blind.

In this story taken from The Gospel According to John, Jesus identifies Himself as the Light of the world. Wherever His Light shines and is received, there is sight. Those who experience His Light are empowered to see the activity of God in their own lives, as well as the world around them.

In his letter to the Ephesians, Paul tells those folks that "once you were Darkness, but now you are Light." He goes on to instruct them to "live as children of the Light."

We can have 20/20 vision and still be blind to what God is doing in our lives. Spiritual vision comes from the Lord, who is able to lift the blindness from our eyes so that we may discover something about the love, grace, mercy, compassion and forgiveness of God and ultimately about our potential to live as children of the Light.

35

Recovering from a Stall

When I was growing up in Spartanburg, SC, one of my friends owned an airplane. It had two seats and one engine. My friend flew back and forth from Spartanburg to the University of South Carolina following Interstate I-26. In fact, the top speed of his plane was about 85 miles an hour, so he flew to the side of the Interstate, because the cars below were going faster than he was flying.

On several occasions I went up with him to take a tour of Spartanburg and the surrounding area from the air. It is certainly a different view of the world from up there. I remember asking him what would happen if the plane stalled out.

He informed me that this procedure was the first thing he was taught, even before he was taught how to land the plane. I wondered, "Why?"

Well, he had a simple response, "If you can't recover from a stall, you don't have to worry about how to land the plane, because it will land itself and maybe in a way that might not be in your best interest."

I was rather glad that he had this procedure under his belt, and would know what to do if it happened to us—which I am happy to say it never did.

One of the most noted spiritual stall-outs is that of the "Prodigal Son." This parable, located in Luke 15, gives us a picture of a spiritual life stalled out. A young man requests his inheritance and then leaves for a far country, where he wastes all that he has. The only work he is able to find is in a pigpen. This is the bottom point of his life.

At this point he comes to his senses; he has a "teachable moment." He is now open to doing something different with his life. He has decided to return to his father's place and be a servant. But when he is yet a far distance away, his father spots him and runs out to meet him.

The Prodigal allows himself to be embraced by his father, and that makes all the difference in the world. The embrace says, "You are accepted, you are wanted, you are loved, and you are forgiven." It brings the wayward son out of his tailspin, which was headed toward spiritual death. As the Psalmist says, "He is soaring with the eagles."

Recovering from a spiritual stall out is the process of moving back toward the Father, and allowing our Father to embrace us and to ensure us that we are safe and okay in His arms. The words of Jesus come to mind here as He spoke to His people who had experienced similar spiritual descents. He says, "Jerusalem! Jerusalem! How many times would I have embraced you as a hen embraces her chicks, but you would not."

Our Heavenly Father is able to lift us up where we belong and allow us to soar with eagles.

36

Slavery or Freedom

Once upon a time in a faraway land, there lived a young king. He decided one day that the kingdom needed a good cleaning up, so he called his servants together and sent them out to do some spring cleaning. All the public buildings were to be cleaned from top to bottom. Working in the public temple, the servants came across an old letter. Although they did not know everything it meant, they had an idea it was very important and took it to the king.

As the king read the letter, he began to cry. His servants were somewhat puzzled. "What did the letter say that had caused this outburst?" they wondered. After regaining his composure, the young king called all the people in the kingdom to come to the palace. Standing before the people, he began to recount the contents of the letter.

A long time ago, their ancestors had been slaves in a faraway land. They were held captive by a very strong nation. There was little hope that they would ever be free again, but the mighty hand of God intervened to set them free. Yes, God had delivered them in spite of the overwhelming odds. They were free not because of their great military might, but because God had delivered them. They had not earned their freedom; it was a gift from God.

As the king looked around his kingdom, he realized that very few people showed any gratitude to God for His gift of freedom. Most people, including the young king, had taken their freedom for granted. They acted as though it were a permanent possession, and not something that could be taken away. Their theology had become "We are the masters of our destiny."

The people were called upon to acknowledge this gift of freedom from God. They were to accept the responsibilities of being a free people in the Lord, which meant that they were not to be slaves to the way of the world, but to the ways of God. They had been set free to reflect God's image in the world, which consists of love, compassion, and forgiveness.

Over in the New Testament, in the Epistle of I Peter 2:9-10, we have our reminder of our past, present, and future from God's point of view.

"But you are a chosen generation, a royal priesthood, a holy nation, a peculiar people; That you should show forth the praises of Him who called you out of darkness into his marvelous light: which in time past you were not a people, but you are now the people of God: which you had not obtained mercy, but now you have obtained mercy."

Again the emphasis is upon the intimate relationship and calling we have from God. We have entered into this exceptional communion with God, which brings lasting obligations. We are to live out our calling, the higher calling of God in Christ Jesus.

It has been said that when Christ calls us, He calls us to come and take up our cross. The freedom that Christ gives to us is to come and die with Him. Die to self! Die to the ways of the world that contradict the will and purpose of God for our lives. Bottom line, it is the freedom to be "a servant of the Lord," not in doing anything and everything we desire to do, but to say, "Not my will, but Thy will be done." This Is Freedom at Its Best!

37

When Smaller Is Better

The same week that I graduated from seminary, a small rural church in Caesar, Nc, was saying good-bye to their pastor. The Reverend Baumgartner had come out of retirement at the tender age of 88 years to pastor this church. Several years before, the church had experienced a split in its congregation. More than three-fourths of the congregation had left the church over denominational issues. It was only by the grace of God that they had a building in which to meet.

Early June was the time for Vacation Bible School at Zoar Baptist. On the final day of this event, Reverend Bumgarner and one of the men from the church went to town to pick up some supplies. Upon their return, Reverend Bumgarner got out of the car, took about three steps and fell to the ground with a massive heart attack. He was pronounced dead on the scene.

Shortly thereafter, I received a call asking me if I were available to provide pastoral ministry for the church. I agreed to do this only for a short time, but ended up staying there three years. Initially, I had bigger plans than to pastor a congregation of 25 to 30 people, but God had other plans for me.

Whatever vocation we decide to take up, we have to start somewhere. While some people seem to have the advantage of starting at a more opportune place than others do, sometimes smaller is better.

We live in a world that has its eyes on the corporate ladder. Moving on up is the goal and motto of those who hope to find fulfillment at the top of the ladder. I don't say that this is wrong, but sometimes smaller is better.

It seems to me that the higher up one goes, the less time there is for personal things, like family, friends and hobbies. Success in the upper ranks has its price. Sometimes smaller is better.

Isaiah 40: 29 says that the Lord gives power to the weak (smallest on the social, economic scale) and to those who have no might (those in positions with no power or authority). He increases their strength (He uses them to accomplish His purpose). That is, He is able to use the weak to extend His presence in the world. Sometimes smaller is better.

The Apostle Paul in First Corinthians says that God has chosen the foolish things of this world to put to shame the wise (those who think they are wise in all things) and God has chosen the weak (small on the social and economic scale) things (people) of the world to put to shame the mighty (those who think they are strong and secure).

In His "Sermon on the Mount," Jesus tells His audience that "Blessed are the poor in spirit, for theirs is the kingdom of heaven." This beatitude has often been understood that Jesus was talking about those who recognize their poor spiritual condition.

Yet another view understands this beatitude as meaning that those who give their life away (become poor in spirit) shall experience the fullness of God. Jesus not only taught His disciples to do this, He was their model of being poor in spirit. This is when smaller is better.

38

Surrounded by the Police

The local AM radio station, WORD, had announced all week that no fireworks would be allowed inside the city limits of Spartanburg on Halloween. There would be a $25.00 fine if you were caught with or using fireworks on that day.

So what did my friends and I do for Halloween that year? We bought fireworks and went to downtown Spartanburg, S.C., at about 7:00 p.m. After a stroll down the main street and setting off a few firecrackers, M-80s to be exact, in a trash-can or two, we saw no sign of any police anywhere around. It was decided that we would go back to the car and head down to the Beacon Drive-In Restaurant to see who was cruising that night.

Everyone had gotten into the car, except Ronnie Danner. Since we were parked on a vacant lot between two three-story buildings, Ronnie thought it would be a good idea to toss an M-80 on top of one of the buildings. Our attempts to dissuade him from doing this fell on deaf ears. He lit the M-80 and threw it toward the top of the building. Up and up went the M-80 until it almost reached the top, but not quite. So, on its return trip, the M-80 exploded about halfway down, and the noise from the explosion, sounded like a cannon.

By the time Ronnie had gotten back into the car, we were surrounded. They came from all directions! There was no escape route! We were trapped!

All the police in Spartanburg were descending on us. They came down on us like flies on honey. Everyone in the car with fireworks dumped them on the floor. I must confess that I did not have one firecracker on me, nor did I bring any with me, but my friends were loaded down with M-80s.

The police had us get out of the car and into a police car and took us to the city jail, where we were fingerprinted and put in a holding cell. Bob Solesbee, one of my friends, had dressed up in his mother's old dress and one of her wigs. The problem was that Bob's mom was about five feet tall and Bob was around six feet tall. His mother's dress looked like a mini-dress on him.

When Bob walked into the cell, he got the attention of all the other cellmates. Eventually, one by one, our parents began to show up to pick up their prodigal sons. My mom showed up around 1:00 a.m. When I came out to meet her, she did not have a pleasant look on her face. I tried to explain that I was innocent, but the way it came off, it certainly looked as though I had been involved in the fireworks violation.

For me, it was being in the wrong place with the wrong

people. As soon as I found out that everyone had fireworks but me, I should have opted out, but I didn't. It cost me $25.00 of my hard-earned money and a temporary mark against my record with the police.

Fortunately for me, this brush with the law did not leave a permanent record. Not so with most prisoners throughout the state and nation. With a felony, there a number of limitations that stay with them for the remainder of their lives when they come out of their incarceration. Not being allowed to vote is one of the restrictions. Hospitals will not hire convicted felons. Some rental properties are off limits to them due to their record.

It seems our society makes it rather difficult for people to put their mistakes behind them. This reminds me of Nathaniel Hawthorne's book, *The Scarlet Letter*, in which Hester was made to wear the letter "A" sewn to her clothing as a reminder to her and the community that she had committed adultery.

Those who have spent time in prison have been stripped of more than their freedom; they have lost a sense of their humanity, self-worth and value. They are made to feel like second-class citizens. They fight an uphill battle trying to re-integrate themselves into the main line of society.

Many are seen as damaged goods, not to be trusted under any circumstance. While we may not have a lot of influence over public opinion, and the laws of the land, we have a choice as to how we relate to such folks. We may shun them or we may choose to have compassion for them. To have compassion means to take action, not to just have a sentimental thought.

In Matthew 25:36 and 40, Jesus says to His disciples, "I was in prison, and you visited Me."

To this statement, His disciples ask, "When did we do this, visit you in prison?"

Jesus responds, "When you do this for the least of God's people, you have done it also to Me."

In the eyes of our Heavenly Father, there is no mistake that He cannot handle. The world can place upon some of its people some very heavy loads that are most difficult to carry.

39

Target Practice Gone Bad

It was that time of year again, when my Army Reserve Unit out of Hickory, N.C., made its annual trip to the firing range to conduct annual weapons qualifications. This year, a site in Statesville used by local law enforcement officers had been selected.

The Line Officer ensures that everything is set in order and that the targets are in place. Each soldier gets an opportunity to adjust the sight on his weapon by firing some practice rounds at the target down range. Soldiers take a look at the shot pattern on the targets and make adjustments on the sights as needed.

This process was going along okay until one of the officers suggested that the chaplain have a go at it. I protested that by the Geneva Convention, chaplains do not carry weapons, nor are they allowed to fire a weapon under any circumstance. Well, a couple more officers got involved. The next thing I knew, I was being handed an M-16, which I was told had been zeroed and was ready to fire. All I had to do was get in a prone position, aim at the target, and pull the trigger.

Against my better judgment, I took the weapon, got down in the prone position and took aim at the target down range and slowly squeezed the trigger. One shot rang out. At the other end of the firing range, a small wire that held up all the targets split. Like the walls of Jericho, all the targets came tumbling down.

The Line Officer immediately snatched the weapon from my hands and instructed me to never fire a weapon again. I had missed the mark and hit the wire holding the targets up. Amazing that I would do that with just one shot!

I am reminded that the core meaning of the New Testament word for "sin" is "missing the mark." In spite of having some of the best instructors plus a weapon that had been zeroed and was ready to fire, I still missed the target.

The Apostle Paul writes in the Letter to the Romans that everyone has missed the mark in life. Not a one of us has been on target. We need someone to help get us back on target, which we can't do by ourselves.

Christ has done for us what we can't do for ourselves— hit the target. He, and He alone, has lived life to the fullest and in perfection to the will and purpose of His Father Who sent Him.

His perfection at hitting the mark is made available to us, though we have not hit it or even come close to it. This is God's grace and mercy, that while we were yet sinners (missing the mark), Christ died for us, so that we could be on target for the Lord.

40

The Prodigal Finds Himself

Two years after high school, I joined the Air Force. This had been a dream of mine throughout high school. Now it was a reality! It was quite an adventure for me to be away from home and on my own.

Very soon in my Air Force life, I took up with the Romans. You know, when in Rome, do as the Romans do. My way of life had become far removed from what it had been back home. I extended some bad habits that I brought with me, like drinking and smoking more and staying out a lot later than I should. Back home I had been a regular at church, but in the Air Force, I seldom went at all.

When I was stationed at Alconberry AFB in England, there seemed to be something going on every night. On Fridays, Saturdays and Sundays, a local band played at the Airmen's Club, and four or five buses full of "birds" (the English word for girls) were at the club to join the fun. On Tuesdays and Thursdays, we went over to the RAF (Royal Air Force) Base to meet more birds and enjoy the bands.

There was one bird who was such a regular at the Airmen's Club that we promoted her to the title, Airman Jenny. It was Airman Jenny who told me one day that I looked bad. I went back to the barracks and took a look for myself, and sure enough, she was right, with bags beneath my eyes, I did look bad. But that did not change my way of life at that time; it just slowed me down for a while.

Eventually, I was discharged from the Air Force and went back home to Spartanburg, SC. The few prayers I said during my Air Force days were that if God would allow me to survive the Air Force, when I got home I would try to do better. Of course, back in Spartanburg, I had forgotten my promise.

It was easy to see I had not left the rowdy life behind, but had, in fact, brought it back home with me. One day I was having lunch with a friend at a local restaurant, and he made a comment concerning a group of young men nearby who were drinking and using very bad language. His words hit me square between the eyes when he said, "The Devil doesn't have to worry about those guys; he has them in his back pocket." Wow! Ouch! The words meant for someone else were very painful for me. I sort of realized that was where the Devil had me.

I went home determined that I didn't want to be in the Devil's back pocket. In the privacy of my room, I asked God to help me get back on track. I accepted responsibility for the life I had lived in the Air Force and had brought home with me. I asked the Lord to renew His spirit in me and to let His forgiveness embrace my life. I started back to church and became involved in the various activities there. My fellowship with other Christians allowed me to receive the support and encouragement I needed to heal my spiritual wounds. I was empowered to leave the old Air Force life behind me and to be open to the new possibilities before me. I continued to discover how God was active in my life and His call for me to become active in His life. Through this process I continued to discover who I was in light of the life that God called me to. That has been many, many years ago, and I am still in the process of discovering who I am in light of what God is doing through me.

41

The Shoes Don't Fit

In a small village far, far away, there lived a family of modest means. The nine children would pass their clothes down from the oldest to the youngest. John was the youngest and was the last in line to receive clothes and shoes from his older brothers.

When his brothers who were several years older outgrew a pair of shoes, John was happy to have them and wore them everywhere he went. He soon developed some painful blisters on his feet. At first, he thought it was just part of the process of getting adjusted to his older brother's shoes, but it got worse. Eventually it so was difficult for him to walk that he stopped going anywhere. His mother noticed this and got him an appointment at the Cobbler's Shop to have his shoes fixed.

The cobbler tried multiple ways to make the shoes work, but to no avail. He talked to John's mother about a new pair of shoes. It seemed to be the only thing left to do, so she agreed. Several weeks went by, and finally a note from the Cobbler's Shop indicated the shoes were ready.

John was very excited about this and could not wait to pick them up. Together, he and his mother went to see the cobbler. John tried on the shoes, and, surprisingly enough to him, they felt great. As he wore them more and more each day, the pain in his feet, legs and back went away.

John was able to run, jump and climb without any pain at all. He found it much easier to do the tasks assigned to him by his mom and dad. Before, he had complained a lot about the work he was asked to do and how difficult it was to complete these various tasks and duties. Who would have thought that new shoes would have done the trick?

One day Jesus found himself surrounded by people who were carrying heavy burdens. Many of them had made home-style yokes that would allow them to carry two buckets of water and other items for great distances. Unfortunately for them, the homemade yokes did not fit very well, so callouses were being formed on their shoulders and they were suffering a lot of pain in their backs. Many of them had come to the point that they needed a lot of help from family and friends just to move small distances. To them Jesus speaks these words found in Matthew 11:28-30 "Come unto me, all you that labor and are heavy laden, and I will give you rest. Take my yoke upon you, and learn of me; for I am meek and lowly in heart: and you shall find rest for your souls. For my yoke is easy, and my burden is light."

Here is what Jesus is offering! He is offering a "yoke" that is made just for you. The "yoke" that He has for you fits you and no one else. The "yoke" He makes for you is just right for you to do whatever tasks or duties He calls you to do.

Homemade yokes never work properly! But the yokes

that the Carpenter's Son makes are perfect for each and every person who wears them. We tend to put more unnecessary stuff on our platter, but our Lord gives us exactly what we can do and do well with His patented yoke.

We can never go wrong wearing His yoke, because it is the yoke that allows us to function at our very best in life. Yokes, like shoes, need to be a perfect fit; our Lord knows the exact size we need.

42

The Short Life of Ernie Hawkins

It was early one Saturday evening that summer when Ernie's parents bought him a new go-kart. Although it was getting dark, Ernie's parents let him make a few trips around the house, which ended with a collision with the clothesline post. No damage to man or machine! Back in the driver's seat, Ernie determined to make another attempt of circling the house, and then halfway around, he decided the heavily traveled street near his home would be the ideal place to see what this machine would do.

So, the next sound that we heard from Ernie's backyard was the go-kart making its way down Williams Street. With no lights or reflectors on his go-kart, Ernie was a prime candidate for being run over by a car or truck. Two or three cars quickly sped away from Ernie's home in an attempt to catch up with him before he was killed by oncoming traffic. They caught up with him near the Salvation Army Youth Center, about a half-mile down the busy street.

This is how Ernie lived much of his life, just doing whatever came to mind, with very little thought to consequences. On one occasion, a small group of us had gathered at the local convenience store. It seems that someone in the group was falsely bragging about going around the curve coming out of the local junior college at 45 mph. Later that evening, Ernie drove his parents' car around the curve at 50 mph and centered one of the concrete posts that marked the entrance to the school. The car was a total loss, and Ernie escaped with a few scratches and bruises.

One Saturday afternoon many years later, Ernie was playing poker with some friends. After losing a considerable amount of money, he left and came back with a gun and started shooting. Someone in the group fired back, and Ernie was killed.

There is a saying that goes something like this:

> Sow a thought, reap a deed!
> Sow a deed, reap a habit!
> Sow a habit, reap a way of life!
> Sow a way of life, reap a destiny!

In the "Sermon on the Mount," Jesus taught his disciples that "blessed are those that mourn, for they shall be comforted" (Matthew 5:4). This Beatitude refers to those who have taken a serious look at their brokenness, hurt, and pain and instead of denying its existence have laid claim to it. This process of facing our brokenness head-on, is what it means to "mourn." It is through this process of "mourning" that one is healed.

After his baptism, we are told that Jesus went into the desert and was tempted for a period of time. After this ordeal, we are told that angels came and ministered unto

Him. In other words, His healing came from above, from God the Father. In the desert Jesus dealt with His fears, uncertainties and doubts about the mission before Him. He did not deny them, but laid claim to them and, therefore, experienced the healing that comes only from God. He came out of the desert a person at peace with himself and at peace with God. Because he had embraced all that was troubling Him deep within His being, He experienced the healing and comfort that would empower His life to be a channel of healing for others. This is the process of mourning spoken of in the second Beatitude.

Unfortunately, Ernie never dealt with his brokenness; he only acted out of it. The Good News is that healing is available to all of us. Instead of acting out of our brokenness, we can bring a healing presence into our world that will be a blessing to us, as well as to those who cross our pathway.

43

The Worst Student

The 6th grade started off fairly well for me. I had Mrs. Edwards as my teacher that year. Since Ruth Elementary School was the smallest school in the state of North Carolina, one class contained all the sixth-graders. All my best friends were in the class, so it seemed as though it would be a good year for me. Not to be!

A couple of my friends and I were always playing tricks on one another. One of the tricks that we played was to sneak up behind another person, and kneel down on all fours, and then Michael or Jimmy would push the person backwards. The poor kid would tumble over and end up on the classroom floor. Sure someone could have gotten hurt, but we were 6th graders, so getting hurt was not something that we thought about.

This trick was played on me so many times that I could not keep count. It took two students to pull that trick off, and, usually, I was out numbered. My way of handling these matters was simply to get up and wrestle the person who had pushed me to the classroom floor. Here is where my problems started. Every time that I would retaliate, in walked Mrs. Edwards. She would see me in the process of grabbing my friend who had just pushed me backwards. I can remember her words like she said them today, "Bob, what you are doing?"

Unfortunately for me, I never had a chance the entire year to tell my side of the story. The most I was allowed to say was "But, but Mrs. Edwards." This scenario repeated itself over and over again throughout the year. No one was caught pushing me; it was always me getting caught pushing back.

As a result, I failed "Conduct" every grading period and therefore failed "Conduct" for the entire school year. Mrs. Edwards informed my parents that in all her many years of teaching school, I was the only student she ever had who failed "Conduct" for the entire year.

After I finished seminary at Southeastern Theological Seminary and had been ordained as a minister, I went back to the school to tell her that I had not turned out all that bad in life. Unfortunately for me again, Mrs. Edwards had retired. I wish that I could have redeemed myself with her, but it did not happen. She would never know what God could do with a renegade 6th grader who failed "Conduct" for the entire year.

It is easy to give up on folks who don't measure up to our standards. We simply write them off as troublemakers with no future. The Good News is that this is not how God sees those of us who have some failures under our belts. Unlike a lot of people in this world, God is able to look beyond our faults and see our potential. He is able to pick up the broken pieces of our lives and put things back together again and again and again. There is no limit to His ability to do this. There is no limit to His willingness to do this. God has always been in the business of taking the worst of humanity and accomplishing His will and purpose. The bottom line? Don't give up on yourself; God isn't through with you yet.

44

Truth Has Consequences

The story goes that Mrs. Jones never missed a Sunday at Waterside United Methodist Church, located near the coast of eastern North Carolina. She was as faithful as the morning sun. Each Sunday after the worship service, she would tell the minister what a good sermon she had preached.

On one particular Sunday, the minister preached on the evils of tobacco and its effect on health issues when smoked, chewed or dipped. After the sermon Mrs. Jones took the minister's hand and politely said, "You've quit preaching and gone to meddling now." It seems the sermon had hit too close to home.

A good friend of mine from seminary was called to my home church in Spartanburg, SC. Grace Baptist would be considered a suburban church, located just on the outskirts of the city of Spartanburg. It had been formed back in the mid-50s as a mission church from Southside Baptist on South Church Street.

The population around the church for the most part was WASP (White Anglo Saxon Protestant), but when Reverend John Paine came along there were changes going on in the community. The Black American Community was growing, as were the Hispanic Community and the Hmong-Laotian Community.

Reverend Paine put forth a proposal to the church about its future endeavors in ministry. One consideration was to stay in the current community and develop a ministry that would meet the needs of the various cultural groups represented. If this proved not doable for the congregation, then the next option would be to move to a new location that would be predominantly WASP. He encouraged the church to go one way or the other.

Well, this created quite a stir in the congregation. A group of members produced a document that opposed doing anything. They were happy with the way things were and did not want to turn the church into a multi-cultural community. Moving away from the present location was out of the question.

The final decision from all the discussion was that the minister must go, since he had caused this entire ruckus. So the minister was asked to leave the church. He became the proverbial "scapegoat." No one thought to ask if perhaps the minister might have been speaking something of the Word of the Lord, and perhaps this was God's will. He was branded as a troublemaker, sent on his way, and the church returned to normal operations.

This is an example of how difficult it is for individuals and for groups to embrace the truth of God's will and purpose. It is just as difficult to embrace the truth about us. Saint Augustine, one of the most prominent early

Church Fathers, wrote in his book, *The Confessions of Saint Augustine*, that the most difficult journey in his life was the journey into the truth of who he was.

The truth about God is that He is a Father who loves His children unconditionally. He is the Father who seeks to embrace His children with His love, grace and mercy. At the heart of our heavenly Father is the desire not to punish us, but to embrace us and all the people around us.

The truth about us is that we have a desperate need to be embraced by our heavenly Father. We need his grace, mercy, and forgiveness, which enable us to embrace His will and purpose for our life and community.

It is difficult for us to let go of that which is familiar to us and to embrace a new direction. There is always some element of the FUD Factor (fear, uncertainty, and doubt) present in God's call to do something different with our lives.

In Genesis chapter twelve, Abraham is faced with God's call to leave his hometown and go where he had never been before. There are certain risks that we must be willing to take in order to embrace the new thing that God wants to do with us.

Change is difficult, and God knows that! Another truth of our heavenly Father is that He is a patient God, ever seeking to bring us from where we are today to where we need to be tomorrow. He sees the possibilities in our lives. He is aware of what we can be and what we can become. The truth of our heavenly Father is that He is able to look beyond our faults and see our needs and our potential. Embracing the truth of God's will for our lives has consequences.

45

Waiting & Waiting & Waiting

It was late in the evening in February of 1988, when I got a call from my mother that my father was in the hospital with a heart attack. Soon I was on my way to Spartanburg Regional Medical Center and a "tour of duty" in the "waiting room," a place filled with anxious people, all waiting for news from the doctors about their family members. Some would be given good news and some bad news.

Little did I know that this would be my first of a series of trips to the hospital and eventually to the waiting room. My father had CHF (Congestive Heart Failure), which required numerous trips to the ER (Emergency Room). I soon discovered that waiting is a most difficult thing to do. At the end of the day, I was worn out from the stress and tension this sort of waiting produces.

Waiting takes different forms, such as: a parent who waits for a son or daughter to make it safely home after an evening out with friends; the waiting that follows a job interview; a person in the military stationed overseas waiting for orders to come home; children waiting for Christmas to come to see if their wishes come true! Waiting seems to be a part of life, and a one that not many like to do.

Rather than the interlude and asking the unknowing question, "What is God doing with me during this time of waiting?" we ask the other question, "Why is God taking so long to answer my prayer?"

Waiting invites us to enter into God's time. We operate under what is known in the Koine Greek as "chromos time," which passes with each second, minute, hour, day, month and year. But God operates out of "kairos time," which is described in the scriptures as "one day is as a thousand years and a thousand years is a day to the Lord."

Another aspect of waiting that we should be aware of is that while we may be inactive during this interlude, God is not. He is actively preparing us for the journey ahead. Since we don't know what will be required of us as we journey through life, waiting is that time when we are encouraged to "be still and become aware of God's presence made available to us."

Worrying is another downside to waiting. The saying goes, "Don't tell me worrying doesn't work; half the things I worry about never happen." Remember, it takes energy to worry, and if we spend the entire waiting time worrying about things we have no control over, what sort of energy will we have when it comes time to move on down the road? So, the mandate from the Lord, as recorded in Isaiah 40:31, is: "Those that wait upon the Lord shall renew their strength. They shall mount up with wings like eagles.

They shall run and not be weary. They shall walk and not faint."

Isaiah penned these words to his people who were held captive in a foreign land. The people wanted to know when the Lord was going to liberate them and bring them back home. How long was it going to be before they received help?

The period of waiting invites us to trust God and His ability to handle our life situation. The possible discovery for us is that our hope of being liberated from our fears, uncertainties, and doubts about our future is more about God's activity than our activity. May God be with you in your waiting!

46

Which Way Is Home?

I had been in Germany for less than two weeks and was assigned to the Ray Barracks Post in Freiburg. A large sign across the top of the gate informed all that entered that this was the former Army home of Elvis Presley. This is where he met Priscilla.

I was in charge of the Ray Barracks Chapel, where all the religious activities took place. My battalion headquarters was located in Giessen, which was about 35 miles away from where I lived in Bad Nauheim. My battalion was having a reception for the chaplains and chaplain assistants who had recently arrived. It was to be at the Chinese Restaurant in Linden, which was four or five miles from Giessen.

I was given the directions on how to get there and arrived with no problems. We had a great time meeting the other staff members and enjoying the delicious food. We finished up around 10:00 pm in the evening, said our good-byes and drove off into the night.

Getting back on the autobahn was no problem, so cruising along I noticed that I did not remember seeing this part of Germany before. A few more miles down the road and I was convinced that I did not have a clue where I was at the time. Not a clue! I was lost with a gas tank that was getting low.

I kept driving and driving around and through the city of Giessen and still could not find a sign that would give me a clue on how to get back to my apartment in Bad Nauheim. After an hour of this, I became a little anxious over the gas issue. If I ran out of gas, no one would ever find me. What would I do? Finally I stopped and asked for help from the Great Navigator. "Lord, I need your help in getting home. I don't have a clue where I am and the road I need to take. Help me find the road I need to take to get back home. As you can see, I'm about out of gas, so I don't have a lot of room for error."

The prayer worked! Somehow I found myself back in Freiberg and Ray Barracks, and from there I made my way to my apartment in Bad Nauheim. It was a long and stressful night, which I hoped not to repeat anytime soon.

Being lost in the "far country," as was the "Prodigal Son," and not knowing how to get back home may be a blessing rather than a curse. Sometimes we need to leave home in order to find home. The "far country" or, as it is often referred to the "desert experience," has a way of bringing life down to the basics. It may create a "teachable moment" that allows us to discover something about ourselves and something about how God is at work in our lives.

Since my days in Germany, I have purchased a GPS device that helps me find my way around in unfamiliar places. Most of the time it works for me! The other system that works 100 percent of the time is God's Positioning System. It seems to always get me from where I am to where I need to be, and that is an ongoing adventure with God.

47

Who Was That Masked Man?

It was a very pleasant day in March and a perfect day to be outside. While I was standing on a corner in downtown Hickory talking with a couple of friends, a stranger approached us from out of nowhere. He was from out of town and was looking for the Catholic Church. We made an attempt to explain to him where the church was, but each effort became more complicated than the other. Eventually, I said that I would take him there. He agreed, and on the way over told me that he had not eaten in a couple of days and that he was homeless and very hungry.

As we looked for a place for him to eat, several options came to mind. Upon seeing a Lowes Grocery Store sign, he said that he would like to go there. I pulled in front of the store and told him that I would give him some money to buy food, but that I wanted one thing from him. He indicated that he didn't have anything to give me, but I responded, "Yes you do."

"What do I have that you want" was his reply.

"Your blessing," was my answer.

He was puzzled, because he felt that his life had been more of a curse to people than a blessing. "You still have the power to bless me," I answered. "Think, what is it you would like to see God to do in my life," I continued.

"To continue being the person you are and caring for people who need help," he replied.

"Thank you for your blessing, you have made my day," I responded.

"And now, may the peace, grace, and mercy of God be with you, and may you always know that you have the power to bless," I continued.

We do not get to choose the person or the place to be blessed of God. God makes those choices! This encounter with a stranger reminds me of the Old Testament story found in Genesis 14: 18 – 20, where Melchizedek shows up at the home of Abraham and blesses him and then rides out of town. After receiving his blessing from this stranger, Abraham presents him with a tithe. Melchizedek is not a Hebrew, but belongs to another religious group, yet he blesses one of the most prominent persons in the Old Testament.

We never know how and when and through whom God may choose to bring a blessing into our lives. The writer of Hebrews says that we should "not forget to entertain strangers, for by so doing some have unwittingly entertained angels." The point is that every human life has potential. Unfortunately, those folks who are down and out are seen as parasites by many and an embarrassment by others, whose solution is to keep them off the streets and out of sight. Merchants fear that this kind of folks will keep customers away and eventually destroy their businesses.

What if God is in these people? What if God is trying to speak to us through these people who are down and out? Perhaps as they come to us with hardly anything but the clothes on their back, they symbolize how we ought to approach God. Perhaps our problem is that we are too full of ourselves and there is no room for God in our "inn." Perhaps the message is similar to the one found in the Gospel According to Matthew 11:28-29: "Come unto Me, all you who labor and are heavy laden, and I will give you rest. Take My yoke upon you and learn of Me, for I am gentle and lowly in heart, and you will find rest for your souls. For My yoke is easy and My burden is light."

The close of the early radio and television show the "Lone Ranger" featured the main character riding off on his white horse, with someone asking, "Who was that masked man?" The stranger who has the potential to bless our lives may very well be the person whom we so often overlook. Lewis Grizzard gives expression to this thought in his book *Shoot Low, Boys – They're Riding' Shetland Ponies*. Perhaps the "pot of gold" is not where we are looking, but somewhere we are overlooking. Perhaps just beneath our eyes!

The Bible is clear on this subject. God comes to His people in a variety of ways, seeking to bless our lives, but we so often miss it because we are looking elsewhere. Jesus' words found in the Gospel According to Matthew 23:37 (my paraphrasing) illustrate the point: "O Jerusalem, Jerusalem, you who keep rejecting the ones I send to you to bless you and to bring healing to your life, but you shut them out of your life and miss all that I would love to do for you. I would like to gather you to Myself, as a hen gathers her chicks, but you will not let Me."

48

Wrestling with God on Hogback Mountain

I started smoking cigarettes around the age of fourteen. I had some good role models in that department. My father had smoked as long as I had known him, and my friends were beginning to pick up the habit as well. It was a natural move for me to pick up the habit, too.

I remember the first cigarette I smoked. It was in a field behind our house on Farley Avenue Extension, located near Spartanburg, SC. I lit up the cigarette and took a deep draw and nearly coughed my head off. I refused to listen to my body, which was trying to tell me something about what I was putting into it. I continued to make attempts at smoking until my body finally grew to accept the over 1000 chemicals involved in the process.

My first pack lasted a couple of months. By the time I joined the Air Force at age twenty, I was up to about one pack a week. At the end of my tour of duty, I was up to about two to three packs a week.

Then I took a job with WSPA-TV in Spartanburg, SC., as an engineer atop Hogback Mountain. It was a lonely tour of duty up there. You were by yourself for at least twenty-four hours at a time. If the TV and FM transmitters were working fine, there was not a lot to do, except smoke cigarettes and drink coffee. It wasn't long before I was up to three or four packs a day.

Family and friends noticed that I was overdoing it with cigarettes and tried to get me to stop, but I would not. My general response was that I could stop anytime I wanted to, I just did not want to.

One day before I headed off to Hogback Mountain, my mother handed me a book by Billy Graham. It was an alphabetical listing of various topics on which Dr. Graham would comment. Upon arrival at the transmitter site, I settled down in front of the console with my coffee and my cigarettes. I reached for the book and said to myself, "If ole Billy has something to say about smoking, I might give quitting some serious thought."

Up to this point, it had seemed that more and more people were on me about my smoking. In fact, I had tried to quit on several occasions, but without much success. I had gone for three hours, then a couple of days, then a week or so without having a cigarette. But in each case, I would return to my habit when things got hectic for me.

I slowly made my way to the "S" section of Graham's book. In that section were his comments on smoking. He talked about our bodies being the temples of God and that we ought to treat them that way. His message hit me between the eyes. I was angry at being confronted this way and felt that God was asking me to do something I could not do. It wasn't fair of God to do this to me.

I was not much on praying at the time, but I did offer up a challenge to God. My prayer went something like this: "God, I want You to either give me the strength to quit smoking, or I want You to get off my back."

One item about working atop Hogback Mountain was that in the winter months you did not know when you would get back down if it snowed. So, with this in mind, I always took about four or five cartons of cigarettes with me to work. I went into the bathroom, opened each carton, then each pack, and ran water over the cigarettes, until I had destroyed between four and five cartons.

I walked out of the bathroom and never had the desire to smoke again. What I could not do for myself, God had to do. Looking back now I see how Step One of the AA Model had played out in my life. I had to admit that I was powerless to deal with the habit that had taken control of my life, and only God could act to set me free. What was impossible for me was possible with God.

49

Cruising for a Bruising

Returning from a visit to Statesville, NC, I spotted a Harley-Davidson Dealership, and on the spur of the moment decided to pull in to see their bikes. My sole intention was just to take a look and nothing else, but that's not what happened that day.

As I was looking over the array of bikes, a salesperson approached me. Her initial question was, "Are you interested in buying a bike?" My response was that I was only looking, and that I had not ridden a bike in quite some time. Next I was invited to ride with her around the parking lot to just get a feel of how the bike performed. It felt great! "Are you sure you don't want to try it one time?"

My better judgment would have answered no, but I was not in my better judgment mode that day. So, my response was, "Yes that would be nice!" The response of an idiot! I needed to be on that bike like I needed to be on the meanest bull in the world. But the bike was so beautiful that saying no was not a possibility for me. I had to give it a try, so with some brief instructions, away I went. It all started so well, and then everything fell apart. Somehow the bike got away from me and the next thing I remember was getting up off the pavement.

I should have known that I had been out for a while, because EMS was on the scene. But in my mind I thought that I had just hit the pavement and had gotten up immediately. Not so. Apparently I had been out for about 15 to 20 minutes. My face was bloody, and I was bruised from head to toe. I convinced the EMS folks that I was okay and that I would drive over to my family doctor and have him look me over.

At the doctor's office I came walking in looking like forty miles of bad road. They immediately took me to a room and started their examination. My blood pressure was 210/116. I was in shock! EMS was called again, and this time they took me away. At the ER some staff asked if my wife knew about this. "Lord no, I'm in enough pain as it is. She's going to kill me when she finds out."

Well, the Scripture warns us that "our sins will find us out," and this has been the case for me. While there are some things we can hide from others and even at times from ourselves, we can never hide from God. God knows what's going on in our lives at all times. Our first grandparents thought they would hide from God, but we are told that God came looking for them and found them in some bushes.

I was afraid of facing my wife that day. I knew I had done the wrong thing, and I knew she was going to be extremely angry with me. Which she had a right to be! I did not want to face those eyes of disappointment and disgust. Like everyone else, I long for approval, not rejection.

Our first grandparents discovered God as one Who embraced them and clothed them. God met their needs that day. No angry God that day and no angry God today. In the worst of our decisions, we find God in the midst of our deep valley and profound darkness, as One Who is able and willing to lead us from where we are to where we need to be.

This is the grace and mercy of God, which surpasses all our understanding. God desires the best for us, not the worst He can do to us, never giving up His pursuit to bring us back into the fold! He is truly the God who looks beyond our "bruises and sees our possibilities."

50

Which Way to Turn?

It was a perfect day to ride my bicycle around the Grace Mill Village, located between Rutherfordton and Ruth, NC. I remember riding down a long hill that curved in front of my house and continuing on for another two hundred feet until you reached Johnson's Grocery Store at the bottom.

On this particular day as I rounded the curve in front of my home, I could see someone crossing the road ahead. We seemed to be in perfect sync. I would move to my left at the same time the person ahead, Paul Laughter, would move to his right. This back and forth maneuver went on until I finally decided to hold my position. Unfortunately, this is exactly what the other person in front of me was doing.

Eventually we met head on, which sent me sprawling over my handlebars and onto the awaiting pavement. Paul, one of my schoolmates, was carrying two cartons of empty soft drink bottles that went sailing in all directions.

No broken bones, but a lot of cuts and bruises on both of us. Later that day I went by Paul's home to apologize and to say that I was sorry that I had run over him with my bike. He apologized for getting in my way. So Paul and I remained good friends in spite of our accident.

In life, there are some things that we need to let go of rather than holding onto. Past wrongs that have been committed against us need to be put in file thirteen (the garbage), so that we may live our lives to the fullest.

The Apostle Paul writes in Ephesians 4:26 "to be angry, but sin not; and do not let the sun go down on your anger." It's not a sin to be angry, but in storing it up, we do great damage to ourselves and to others. Anger that is stored up creates a negative energy that impacts everyone around us. It becomes like an infectious disease, which contaminates everyone who comes into contact with it.

The person who gives us the most trouble in life and who can hurt us the most is not the stranger in our midst, but usually a family member, a friend, or a neighbor. These are the folks that we associate with the most and they have the greater capacity of hurting us.

Jesus tells us in his Sermon on the Mount that we ought to love not only our neighbors, but our enemies as well. He knew the destructive nature of anger turned inward and how it can eat away at a person's inner soul. He suggests that we get rid of our anger through the act of forgiveness. Forgiveness is the valve that allows our anger to be released. Like a helium balloon that is released into the wild blue yonder, we are to give our anger back to God.

The questions are: "Which way do we turn? What do we do with our hurt, pain, and anger? Do we turn inward, allowing it to destroy our life, or do we turn it loose and give it back to God?"

One way leads to death and the other leads to life. Which way will you turn?

Afterword

Thank You for Purchasing This Book.

I hope you have enjoyed this book of devotions, and they have encouraged you to look for God in uncommon places throughout your day. Remember, God loves you and wants to be involved in your everyday life and give you life eternal.

If you liked this book, will you do me a favor and leave me a "Customer Review" at Amazon.com where this book is listed? Your review will help others find it and hopefully find God in uncommon places also. Just go to the link below and post your review in the section that says, "Write a customer review."

Just click on this link to leave a customer review:

http://goo.gl/7xS8XB

Wishing You God's Best,

Robert L. Ford

Robert Loran Ford

Robert Loran Ford was born on a cotton mill village in western North Carolina. At age twelve my family moved to Spartanburg, S.C. and soon after high school I joined the Air Force and became a Navigational Specialist. After the Air Force I went back to college to pursue a career in ministry. After college I decided to enter Golden Gate Theological Seminary in Mill Valley, CA. I became Youth Director at Chinese Grace Baptist Church in San Francisco. After ten years in various pastoral roles, I ended up as Director of Pastoral Care at a hospital in Hickory, N.C.

Along the way I switched from the Air Force to the Army and eventually was deployed to Germany as part of a back fill for the First Armor Division which was deployed to Iraq. Eighteen months later I came home to retire from the Army with a Meritorious Service Medal and a Humanitarian Service Medal.

The North Carolina Chaplains Association presented me with the "Chaplain of the Year Award in 2005.

It is hard for me to believe how God has used a shy, introverted person like myself in so many facets of ministry. This is truly Amazing Grace.

You can learn more about Robert at his Author Central Profile Page: http://goo.gl/OwJblv

or

Contact Robert Here: chaplain.hobbit@gmail.com

RESOURCES:

Other Books You Will Enjoy From His Way Publishing:

Holy Desperation: How to Find God When You Need Him Most

http://goo.gl/yYYCJN

Pastor, We Need Too Talk: How Congregations and Pastors Can Solve Their Problems Before it's too Late

http://goo.gl/dM7E13

The Product Hunter's Guide: Finding stuff to resell on eBay, Amazon, Craigslist and beyond

http://goo.gl/T46iBk

Traveling in The Slow Lane: Lessons Learned From Bus People and Ad- ventures Traveling on the Road

http://goo.gl/9nhEDU

Job Skills: Career Success with Self Help and Interpersonal Job Skills http://goo.gl/B7O8Va

BEHIND GRANDMA'S APRON STRINGS

If you are interested in having your book published contact His Way Publishing at:

customerservice.ebooks@gmail.com

www.ingramcontent.com/pod-product-compliance
Lightning Source LLC
Chambersburg PA
CBHW061945070426
42450CB00007BA/1060